"THE STARTING PLACE FOR TRULY KNOWING GOD IS ALWAYS HERE, ALWAYS NOW."

"Although I've pursued intimacy with God for many years, often there are days when I feel as though I'm just beginning to get to know Him. Many days I think, 'How do I live out what I believe today? How can I experience You, God, Who are invisible and glorious?' For me, to 'begin' means being still and silent before God to hear His love words. It means shaking off old thought patterns that would send me into a frenzy of legalistic tasks. It means remembering that when Jesus said 'Abide in Me,' He wasn't telling us to follow a list of strict rules and regulations. He was saying *live with Me, share My life*—get to know Me! It means being reminded that I am His, and He loves me deeply, absolutely."

—FROM *INTIMATE FAITH*

"Winebrenner beckons readers past compulsive Christianized checklists for good behavior to the deep joy of living near the heart of God. . . . Read it and be refreshed."

—BRENDA WAGGONER, AUTHOR OF *THE VELVETEEN WOMAN*

"Jan Winebrenner takes us where women are wanting to go—into the depths of God. . . . Jan beautifully reopens [Christian disciplines] as the meeting places where we can hear, see, know, and feel the heart of the One who knows and loves us intimately. A book to linger with and savor, a book to change your life."

—BECKY FREEMAN, SPEAKER AND AUTHOR OF
MILK & COOKIES TO MAKE YOU SMILE

INTIMATE
FAITH

A WOMAN'S GUIDE TO
THE SPIRITUAL DISCIPLINES

JAN WINEBRENNER

WARNER FAITH

WARNER BOOKS

An AOL Time Warner Company

Unless otherwise noted, Scripture quotations are from the HOLY BIBLE: NEW INTERNATIONAL VERSION®. Copyright 1973, 1978, 1984 by International Bible Society. Used by permission of Zondervan Publishing House. All rights reserved.

Scripture quotations noted NASB are from the NEW AMERICAN STAN-DARD BIBLE®, © Copyright The Lockman Foundation 1960, 1962, 1963, 1968, 1971, 1972, 1973, 1975, 1977. Used by permission.

Scripture quotations noted MSG are from *The Message: The New Testament in Contemporary English*. Copyright © 1993 by Eugene H. Peterson.

Scripture quotations noted KJV are from THE KING JAMES VERSION.

Warner Books, Inc. 1271 Avenue of the Americas, New York, NY 10020

An AOL Time Warner Company

Printed in the United States of America

ISBN 0-7394-3188-9

Book design and text composition by Nancy Singer Olaguera
Cover design by Brigid Pearson

For Ken, who models for me Christ's love
for His Bride, the Church

ACKNOWLEDGMENTS

~

No book is ever written in a vacuum. My life has been filled with people who encouraged me, loved me, and mentored me, the first among whom were my parents. How can I ever thank them for leading me to faith in Christ?

To Ken, my husband, any words of thanks are inadequate. His loving support and encouragement defy all measure.

To my children, Matt and Molly, I can never thank them enough for the lessons in love they have taught me.

To the shepherds at Northwest Bible Church, thank you for your prayerful, humble leadership. To the Grace Class, thank you for your love and prayers.

To my many friends in the Dallas writing community, the Tejas Writers Roundtable and the Dallas Christian Writers Guild, I will always be indebted to you for the generous sharing of your knowledge, experience and camaraderie.

To Alan Elliott, my critique partner, thank you for challenging me to think harder, study more, write better, and pursue excellence.

My hearty thatnks to my agent, Karen Solem, for believing in me and encouraging me.

To the staff at Warner Faith, especially my editor, Leslie Peterson, thank you for your vision and enthusiasm for this project.

If *Intimate Faith* speaks the truth in love to any soul, it is because of the kindness and generosity of these and many others too numerous to mention, who shared out of the wealth of their own lives to enrich mine.

My cup overflows.

CONTENTS

~

INTIMATE
FAITH

1

~

DABBLERS OR DISCIPLES?

When I was a little girl, my dearest dream was to own a horse. When my family moved to the Navajo Indian reservation just as I was starting high school, my dad tried to soften the trauma of uprooting me from my friends with this almost promise: "Maybe I'll buy you a horse." He bought me a motorcycle—a tiny Honda Trail 90. It drank cheap gas and could live by the back door; it didn't need shoes, vet calls, or a trailer for hauling.

I had many great adventures on that Honda, riding over sheep trails and through ravines and canyons that hid secret pools and mysterious rock formations. But my heart was set on owning a horse. Always I pretended I was on horseback, and I never gave up my dream.

The day my husband, Ken, bought me a horse has to be one of my all-time-best days.

I had been taking riding lessons on a chestnut mare named Tess at a little stable in South Carolina. The trainer had mentioned that Tess was for sale, but I never allowed myself to think about buying her. How could we afford her, along with stable costs (we lived in town), farrier and vet bills, not to mention saddles, bits, bridles, and all the rest of the tack I borrowed each time I rode? But every day I fell more in love with this beautiful mare. I learned the basics of caring for her as well as how to walk, trot, and canter, and I pretended she was mine.

Then one afternoon, Ken came home from work and said, "Come take a drive with me."

When we arrived at the barn I asked, "What's up?"

"We're buying a horse today," he said, grabbing my hand and pulling me toward Tess's stall.

I couldn't breathe. And then I couldn't see through a blur of tears. I stumbled into Tess's stall, threw my arms around her neck, and sobbed. Ken stood in the doorway grinning, waiting for me to finally erupt with the laughter of pure joy.

Later that night, I fell asleep with fantasies of the equestrian life galloping through my dreams. I imagined myself riding through fields, jumping Tess over colorful fences, cantering through forests to the accompaniment of baying hounds and squeaking leather.

I never imagined what it would take to make those dreams come true.

Life is often like that, isn't it? We harbor our dreams, sometimes for years, savoring them, but seldom do we really understand what it will take to make them a reality.

When Ken gave me the gift of a horse, I had no idea what I would have to do to become the kind of rider I dreamed of being. I didn't know how much I would have to learn to become proficient enough to ride my horse over a three-foot obstacle, land safely, turn and canter toward the next fence, and complete an entire course. All of this, of course, without taking a fence out of order, pulling a rail, or worse, breaking my neck.

As weeks of riding passed and lessons piled upon lessons,

reality hit me in the chest like a flailing hoof. This riding thing, the whole equestrian thing, the way I wanted to do it, was a full-time endeavor. It was not something I was going to be able just to "pick up."

I noticed that the good riders at the stable where I rode took lessons all the time. They signed up for clinics with world-class trainers. They arrived at the barn early every morning, worked their horses, then studied videos and watched other classes to learn more. They attended horse shows where they competed and others where they just observed. They read books about riding; they studied their horse's "way of going"—I didn't know a horse *had* a "way of going."

I never became the rider I wanted to be. Over time, the demands of family and the limits of budget loomed as more indomitable obstacles than the colorful fences and log jumps that stood in the hunt field. But as I walked away, I took with me some of the most valuable lessons I would ever learn.

The equestrian life I dabbled in for a few years became for me a metaphor of my Christian life.

The Big Five

For many years, I thought that an active, Bible-informed Christian life consisted of the practice of certain daily habits. Every discipleship class I ever attended emphasized the same ones—always five; always the same five: study, prayer, worship, fellowship, and service.

I didn't confuse the discipleship experience with the salvation experience—I knew the Bible well enough to comprehend the difference. I understood that Jesus' death paid the debt of my sin that I could never pay. I knew it was his overwhelming act of grace and mercy that secured my place in heaven and made me a child of God through faith. But discipleship often confused me.

My faith was fragile—the slightest disturbance in my world could send me tumbling into a field of doubts and uncertainties about God's goodness. I didn't have the kind of intimacy with God that my discipleship classes promised. I yearned to know God, to experience his power and presence more fully, yet this kind of relationship eluded me. God seemed distant, strange. I knew his Word, his promises, but for all my knowledge, it seemed I didn't know God.

I practiced some spiritual disciplines—the five most commonly recognized ones. No one would argue that these are basic building blocks for a disciple's life. But I knew I was missing something. Could it be that God wanted to deposit in me vast treasures of grace, if I could only learn to widen my heart? But how? The question haunted me.

Dry, stale, thirsty for God, I began praying that he would show me how to open my heart. I prayed that he would teach me how to move into deeper levels of intimacy with him. I prayed that I would learn how to know God, *really* know him.

I was tired of living a limp, weak spiritual life. I was tired of saying I loved God, when the truth was that I hardly knew him apart from the facts I read about him. I certainly didn't trust him as he deserves to be trusted. I was living proof of Brennan Manning's words: "You will trust God only as much as you love him. And you will love him not because you have studied him; you will love him because you have touched him—in response to his touch."[1]

I yearned for the touch of God. I had no idea how it would happen, but I prayed that his fingers would press on my heart and mark me with the certainty of his presence. In almost immediate response to that prayer, I stumbled into a study of the classical spiritual disciplines.

Over the next few years, I discovered there is much more to the life of discipleship than I had ever imagined. I learned that walking with God involves more than merely doing the four or five things a denomination may teach in a six-week discipleship class.

I learned that the spiritual disciplines are God's means of training us, finite and flawed creatures, to love the invisible, almighty, infinite Creator; they are the means by which we learn to enjoy him; they are the means God uses to nurture our confidence in his goodness and love.

Through the spiritual disciplines God not only touched me, he gripped me hard in a fist that is stronger than a lion's paw.[2] He pulled me close against his heart and taught me to discern the rhythms of grace.

A Great and Precious Irony

As I studied and experimented with the spiritual disciplines, I was struck by this great and precious irony: it is through discipline that grace is best experienced. The Puritan preacher Robert Leighton understood this three centuries ago when he wrote, "The grace of God in the heart of man is a tender plant in a strange unkindly soil."[3]

Legalism and confusion about the true nature of God had made my heart's soil unkind toward grace. The truth of his unrelenting compassion toward me found little welcome in my heart. I was unable to live in the reality of that most essential truth that "being the beloved constitutes the core truth of our existence."[4] But as I began to exercise the spiritual disciplines, the soil of my heart became welcoming, receptive to the sweetness of the gifts of grace.

Through *doing* the spiritual disciplines I began to understand the truth about *being*—being God's beloved child, being the accepted and cherished bride of Christ.

An Offer of Rest

Even as I write this, I am aware of how little I "do," and how much God does for me and has already done for me in sending Christ to redeem me; and all he will continue to do for me throughout my lifetime and into the aeons of eternity.

On the other side of the discussion of "doing," I am aware that we live in an era when most Christians are so busy with activities and programs and family and work obligations that the mere suggestion of "doing more" can trigger guilt, anger, or even a panic attack. So let me put your mind at ease with this word: the spiritual disciplines are not a rigid set of rules imposing stringent behavior practices on us. Nor do they require more tasks and activities added to already overburdened lives. The great beauty offered by the spiritual disciplines is this: they teach us how to rely on the loving sufficiency of God; they show us how to recognize his presence and revel in his sovereignty; they lead us into ever-deepening levels of intimacy with the God who calls us his "beloved"; they teach us to allow God to work for us, in every situation. In short, they offer us rest.

Relating to an Invisible God

I admit I was surprised to discover that there was so much more to the equestrian sport than learning to mount, walk, trot, canter, and dismount. It was daunting at first to realize all that I had to learn. But it didn't take me long to see that the new skills I was acquiring (slowly, sometimes awkwardly) increased my delight in riding. I became more comfortable, more competent in the saddle. I had less trouble staying on course, and my body moved more gracefully, more in sync with my horse. I had more tools for guiding Tess and better aids for negotiating challenging situations, both in and out of the jump ring. Every skill I learned enhanced my love of the sport and increased my pleasure.

In much the same way, I've discovered that learning and practicing the spiritual disciplines has enhanced my spiritual life and shown me how to enjoy God and trust him more fully. They have become training tools that heighten my awareness of God in my daily, moment-to-moment existence; they train me to participate more fully, more consciously, in the kingdom purposes of God; they teach me how to relate to an invisible God.

I have seen my faith grow stronger, my soul enlarged (slowly and often in only small increments) to receive more of his grace and sweetness.

I have come to understand this reality: if all we are doing as Christians, as disciples of Jesus Christ, is practicing a few habits in order to look like a Christian (whatever that looks like), or to satisfy a denominational standard for behavior, we are doing little more than *dabbling* with the idea of discipleship. And instead of reveling in the abundant life Jesus promised us, instead of experiencing increasing intimacy with him and an ever-growing confidence in his goodness, we can expect discouragement, disillusionment, and frequent failure.

The Ancient Paths

For most of us, our Christian traditions encouraged the practice of some of the spiritual disciplines, although which disciplines varied from denomination to denomination. Growing up in a very conservative Christian community, I never heard a sermon on the disciplines of silence or simplicity; however, many a pastor preached study and service. I heard sermons on prayer and worship, but never on humility or celebration or solitude.

My friend Marie grew up in Australia in a religious tradition that emphasized church attendance—just show up. Confession was mandatory, but she never learned about private worship or meaningful Bible study. She never heard a sermon on submission or sacrifice.

As we shared our spiritual heritages with each other, we discovered that both of our traditions had ignored, or forgotten, most of the habits that Jesus taught and lived in front of his followers. Neither of us had ever been taught silence as a discipline, or submission, or sacrifice. No one had ever included the disciplines of fasting or meditation in a discipleship class. Yet down through the centuries, faithful, godly individuals have practiced these disciplines and urged others to follow them as well.

Jeremiah the prophet called: "Ask for the ancient paths, / ask where the good way is, and walk in it, / and you will find rest for your souls."[5]

These disciplines, these ancient paths, when embraced in faith with reliance on the Holy Spirit, are the very means that offer us hope for change and the expectation of spiritual growth. They are our promise of rest and peace.

Lurking Dangers

Two dangers lurk in any discussion of the spiritual disciplines. The first, and the most perilous: thinking that exercising the spiritual disciplines will earn us favor with God and make us worthy of a home in heaven. We must never forget that the disciplines are training tools only, aids that enable us to grab hold of God's promises, to live in the reality of his love and presence, to understand what it means, experientially, to be "in Christ." They do not impart life.

Life comes only through the Son, the Begotten of the Father, who came to show us what grace and truth look like. When we forget this, "the gospel becomes just a pattering of pious platitudes spoken by a Jewish carpenter in the distant past."[6]

John Wesley testified that until he understood grace, the methodical approach through the effort of discipline didn't make sense. But "his heart was strangely warmed" once he found salvation through faith in Christ. He learned that salvation preceded growth toward discipleship.

The second danger is that, having understood salvation, we would misunderstand the purpose of spiritual disciplines. We would try to make them an end in themselves, rather than a means of encountering God and experiencing his presence. We would treat them like rules we force on ourselves and on others, with no relationship to the pursuit of intimacy with God.

Thomas Merton wrote: "An activity that is based on the frenzies and impulsions of human ambition is a delusion and an obstacle to grace. It gets in the way of God's will, and it creates more problems than it solves."[7] The problems we create for ourselves are pride and legalism, defeat and despair.

Those problems multiply when we attempt to force others to get busy about the business of *being good,* without understanding that the only business that matters is that we *be God's.* We become guilty of coercion and manipulation; we become unkind usurpers of the Holy Spirit's work, which is always gentle, courteous, and respectful.

This, then, is our strong reminder: that the bedrock of our faith is Jesus Christ, crucified for our sins, raised on the third day, ever living to intercede for us and bring us into glory. On that foundation we build a life of loving obedience and trust, trained by the spiritual disciplines that Jesus taught and exhibited for us.

Disciplines of Jesus' Life

Even the most casual look at Jesus' life reveals at least fifteen disciplines. Some contemporary scholars as well as some of the classic Christian writers suggest seventeen. We have to ask: if *he* needed the disciplines of solitude, silence, fasting, meditation, secrecy, and the others we've so often and so carelessly ignored, don't we need them too?

That is what this book is about.

It is about the disciplines that characterized Jesus' life—the commonly accepted ones, along with the often unheeded and long-neglected spiritual disciplines. All, I've discovered, are necessary for us to practice if we are serious about intimacy with God, if we are serious about seeing our faith grow strong and unshakable.

In the chapters that follow, we will study, for example, the discipline of humility. Did you know that it is a discipline that you can aspire to, and actually achieve, through the work of the Holy Spirit? A foundational discipline, humility trains us to allow God to work in our lives. It trains us to bow to his authority and recognize his supremacy. It trains us to live peacefully with mystery, trusting God with the unknowns and uncertainties of our lives. It trains us to live among others with gentleness, without the need to dominate, to control, or to manipulate.

We will also examine the disciplines of abstinence,[8] such as fasting, chastity, simplicity, secrecy, silence, and sacrifice. We will see how God uses these in our lives to prove his sufficiency. We will learn the truth of the statement that "God is most glorified in us when we are most satisfied in Him."[9]

A study of the spiritual disciplines must include the five we most commonly associate with an active spiritual life—they are important and must not be deleted as other disciplines are added. But their worth to our spiritual lives will be enhanced as we learn to practice the other disciplines as well, disciplines such as celebration and confession and meditation.

The Principle of Immersion

In his great book *Seeking the Face of God*, Gary Thomas wrote, "The struggle of the Christian life is really a struggle to maintain the centrality of God in our day-to-day lives."[10]

The struggle is perhaps never more real than now. Our world has morphed into a terrifying planet. We live with a level of anxiety and unrest that is unprecedented in our nation's history. How desperately we need to be able to keep God in first place, central to everything we do. But it isn't easy. We are distracted by our fears and disillusioned by our defeats. Even if we've made the decision to "put God first," we aren't sure how to go about it.

Jesus invited us to "remain" in him for safety and comfort, but we're not clear on that either. His call to "abide in me" sounds good, but it too is abstract. We have to wonder: what does "abiding" look like? The spiritual disciplines answer that question. We learn how to keep God central in our day-to-day lives.

Paul wrote, "I pray that the eyes of your heart may be enlightened in order that you may know the hope to which he has called you, the riches of his glorious inheritance in the saints, and his incomparably great power for us who believe."[11] The spiritual disciplines open our eyes to the hope of our faith; they act as guides to scenic views where the riches of our inheritance lay before us in majestic panorama. They show us how to avail ourselves of Jesus' resurrection power.

But above all, as we interact with God and see him work on our behalf, we begin to comprehend the truth of our belovedness. We begin to learn how to live in the reality of the invisible truths of the omnipotent God who calls us to share his life and his eternal kingdom.

Dabbling or Dedicated Disciple?

It has been several years since I last rode a horse over a fence. Even today, I can sit very still and summon the feelings that used to overwhelm me when I cantered across a hunt field. I can feel the rush that filled me as Tess and I turned toward a fence. I see her ears prick forward, feel her hooves lift, and then, for one unfathomable instant, gravity submits to us, and horse and rider fly!

Often on Saturday nights, I watch horse shows on the Outdoor Life Channel. Horse and rider enter the arena and the challenges begin as they soar over stone walls and water jumps, over decorated fences and down steep embankments. I watch with the eye of one who has ridden just a little, just enough to recognize some of the small adjustments that make such a big difference in the outcome of a ride.

I see the tiny movement of a hand as it settles higher on the crest, the almost invisible tightening of a leg against the horse's flank, the little movement on the reins that lessens the pressure on the bit. I see the rider's eyes as she counts strides to place her mount the perfect distance from the fence for takeoff. These, and a dozen more almost indiscernible movements, preoccupy the mind of the rider who will meet the challenges of the course.

The rider whose skills include only the obvious basics—walk, trot, canter, mount, and dismount—would never be able to keep her seat over the first obstacle. She would never ride with the joy and liberty of a more disciplined rider. The exuberance of flight on horseback would be for her an elusive dream, her reality marked by boredom, disappointment, and danger.

The parallels are obvious.

We cannot put limits on our discipleship, choosing only to exercise four or five familiar habits. If we want to walk with God and experience his power in our lives, and grow in knowledge of him and love for him, our only option is this: full immersion into the life of Christ, through the exercise of *all* of the spiritual disciplines.

This was Jesus' plan for us. As he was commissioning his disciples he told them to do and to teach others to obey everything he had taught them.[12] It takes only a cursory look at the life of Jesus to see that he built into his life the consistent practice of many habits. He taught them in his sermons, he practiced them before the disciples and in private hours of fellowship with his Father.

Jesus, fully God clothed in human flesh, saw the need for the disciplines of silence, and simplicity, and fasting, and submission, and the other almost forgotten and ignored habits of heart and hand during his incarnation.

As he exercised the disciplines he testified to his "other-worldliness"; he demonstrated the reality of the kingdom of God; he exhibited his unity with the Father, showing us how to "remain in him," how to live in constant awareness of the Father's deep love.

The practice of the spiritual disciplines does for us what it did for Jesus. The disciplines immerse us in the life of the kingdom. They bring us to the place where we can enjoy intimacy with our Father. They train us to live out the realities of the invisible kingdom Jesus came to display. They strengthen us to withstand temptation. They nurture our spirits here, while we are physically separated from our heavenly Father, and whet our appetites for the things that will truly satisfy us—the things of God, intimacies and realities of fellowship that we will never experience if we only dabble in discipleship.

One Single Duty

These words say it well: "There remains one single duty. It is to keep one's gaze fixed on the master one has chosen and to be constantly listening so as to understand and hear and immediately obey His will."[13]

This is what it means to be a disciple. The spiritual disciplines train us to listen and to understand, to hear and to obey.

Today, in our culture, many of the "ancient paths" seem to have nearly disappeared, but they are there, still, beckoning us with the offer of intimacy with God, of experiential knowledge of his power and love, and the assurance of soul-deep rest and peace.

In the pages of this book, we will dig through the undergrowth to find the ancient paths. We will examine the disciplines that characterized the lives of Old Testament saints, such as Abraham, Esther, David, and others.

We will study these disciplines that Jesus exhibited for us, disciplines that his disciples exercised and taught in the Epistles. We will trace them through the lives of present-day believers, those who falter and fail along with us, yet whose lives speak eloquently of the love and mercy of God, calling us to learn of his grace and discover the joy of his sufficiency.

To Know That God Is Real

Oswald Chambers wrote, "The one thing for which we are all being disciplined is to know that God is real."[14] Nothing is more important. Nothing is more rewarding than discovering that God is everything he said he is: all-powerful, sovereign, yet tender and compassionate, accepting of us in our fragile state, and desiring with all his heart to bring us to rest in him.

Nothing is more important than learning to live in the reality of God's invisible presence.

Equally important is a daily discovery of the liberty of grace and victory over besetting sins. This, wrote Stephen Charnock, is "that which glitters in redemption."[15] Through the exercise of the spiritual disciplines we experience the glory of our redemption, here and now. The sparkle of grace lights our hearts; victory shines through the darkness. We celebrate our redemption with every exercise that brings us into closer harmony with the eternal schemes of God.

If the "glitter" of your redemption has dulled; if you are frustrated and confused about what an "abundant life" looks like; if you're tired of struggling and being defeated; if you're weary with wondering if God is doing his part—join me on a journey through the ancient paths. We will, through the pages of this book, travel "good ways" you may have never before explored. Together we will seek God and find him to be all we could ever need, and more than we ever imagined he could be.

Our map into this extraordinary life: the classical spiritual disciplines.

2

~

"MY LIFE IS IN YOUR HANDS"

THE DISCIPLINES OF SUBMISSION
AND HUMILITY

*M*y teen years on the Navajo reservation were some of my best. I will never regret my father's decision to accept a teaching position at Window Rock High School, near the capital of the Navajo Nation. I loved the land, the people, the freedom of living in a place untouched by the demands and expectations of typical suburban life. It was an adventure I'll always treasure.

I learned to drive my dad's white Ford on the dusty roads that meander through red-rock lands. I learned to watch the bloody practice of sheepshearing at the corral near the trading post and not feel sick. I learned to eat Navajo tacos made with mutton. I learned that skin color means nothing when it comes to friend-ship.

One thing I didn't learn was the language. Except for one badly butchered verse of "I Have Decided to Follow Jesus," I know only four or five words in Navajo. I'm a *biligaana*, an

Anglo, and few of us have ever learned the Navajo language. With its guttural sounds and glottal stops, it is considered one of the most difficult languages on the planet, almost impossible to learn unless you are born to it.

Besides being difficult to learn and speak, Navajo is extremely hard to translate because many English words have no Navajo equivalent. Our word *please* is one of those.

In the native culture, this isn't a problem, because courtesy is communicated with many subtle gestures and mannerisms. Outside the Navajo community, however, beyond the boundaries rimmed by river-forged canyons and tall red spires that look like rockets poised for launch, this missing word has at times caused confusion. In one instance, it was a source of great pain for the children of the *Dinéh*.

It was the late fifties and early sixties. By federal decree, all Native American children were required to attend government-accredited schools. Thousands of young Navajos who lived in remote reservation areas were taken from their families and transported to towns hundreds of miles away to attend school. Yanked from their hogans, they moved into dormitories where Anglo dorm attendants insisted they speak only English. I attended elementary school with many of these children, years before I went to live on their land.

Only years later did I understand what life had been like for them when they were forced to leave their homes and adapt to Anglo ways.

In a sensitive and moving article in the magazine *Arizona Highways*, writer Sam Negri tells how the children were scolded and shamed by dormitory matrons for not saying "please" at mealtime. Baffled, the children didn't understand what they were being ordered to say. Finally, after some research, a linguist suggested that the word "asholdah" might be comparable to the English "please." But those who knew and understood the Navajo people recognized it as a poor substitute.[1]

Not a simple term of courtesy, *asholdah* has no one-word English equivalent. It is better translated, "My life is in your hands."

Navajos don't use "asholdah" lightly. They reserve it only for severe occasions when extreme need is pressing. It is not a word commonly spoken around the dinner table. Yet Navajo children, making a simple request for ketchup at a meal, found themselves speaking the Anglo word "please" while thinking *asholdah* and all that it connoted. The value of their lives was suddenly reduced to the equivalent of a condiment.

Such a tragic misuse of a beautiful word. *Asholdah*—its syllables weep with significance. I have claimed this word for myself, using it often until it has burrowed deep into my spiritual vocabulary. It echoes in my heart daily, many times each day, as I approach the throne room of the King of kings and Lord of lords.

"Asholdah," I whisper. It is the only word that comes to mind when I consider the posture of the creature in the presence of the Creator.

Where Humility and Submission Begin

C. S. Lewis wrote, "What is concrete but immaterial can be kept in view only by painful effort."[2] Oh, how I agree. At times it seems that only by Lewis's "painful effort," by the strenuous exercise of submission and humility, I am able to keep God's magnificent, immaterial majesty in view.

I grasp at the mere edge of a fringe of the hem of the garments that clothe our God in glory. Yet it is the truest truth—

that our God is the ultimate power, the ultimate creative presence, the sole source of life and all manner of matter in this universe, and beyond. And that is the wonder, the majesty of the Christian faith: that our God is of such a superlative sublime nature as to be supreme in every aspect of his being.

And wonder of wonders, beyond even that—he invites us to share in his glory. He welcomes us into his majesty, into his very heart, giving us access through his Son, Jesus Christ. He asks us to call Him "Abba," Daddy.

This great God, full of grace and truth, beckons us into his presence, into the throne room from which he rules the universe, and invites us to enjoy all his unexcelled gifts, all his magnificent power, and to bask in the free-flowing rush of his tender love.

This is our God.

This is our Savior. From this great truth emanates another: my life is in his hands.

Fénelon said it this way: "There are only two truths in the world, that God is all and the creature is nothing."[3]

In the Book of Isaiah, God said of himself:

I AM God.
I alone explain the past and the future.
My purposes will stand, unaltered by any force.
I will do what I please.
I will do what I said I would do.
I will accomplish what I have planned.[4]

Jean-Pierre deCaussade could have been responding to this passage three centuries ago when he wrote, "So we leave God to act in everything, reserving for ourselves only love and obedience to the present moment. For this is our eternal duty. This compelling love, steeped in silence, is required of every soul."[5]

This is where humility and submission begin: we leave God to act in everything. We acknowledge that our lives are in his hands. This is the threshold from which we step into discipleship.

Recognizing God's Mysterious, Transcendent Nature

Ours is not a culture that enjoys mystery, except in a movie or a novel. And then we aren't really happy unless the mystery is solved to our satisfaction. The fact is, we don't mind not knowing if it is only for the first eighty-five minutes of a ninety-minute feature film, or for the time it takes to read a John Grisham or a Mary Higgins Clark best-seller. But as soon as final events tick down in the story, we want certainty. We are impatient with unknowns.

Such is the strength of our culture. We thrive on the tenacity of medical researchers who resist the unknown with every atom of their beings. We build laboratories and think tanks and hire people to examine mysteries and solve them for us. Yet this, what is our very strength as a society, is the fatal flaw of the life of faith.

Faith accepts that there are mysteries that will never be unraveled by the human mind. It accepts that God is transcendent; that much of what occurs on this planet will defy human explanations. It gives up the urgent, human craving to have all the answers, all the time.

"The more comfortable we are with mystery in our journey, the more rest we will know along the way," wrote John Eldredge.[6] The disciplines of humility and submission train us to live joyfully, peacefully, in the realm of divine mystery. They work to strengthen the ligaments and tendons of our knees, often only by "painful effort," until we can bow before God, bending low in the shadow of his transcendence, accepting the unknowns of this life without argument or resistance.

Our Reasonable Response

Of all the things God asks of me, this submission, this humility in response to his transcendence, is the most difficult. Yet of all the things he asks of me, this is the most reasonable.

It is reasonable to bow in humility before the King of kings and Lord of lords, recognizing his authority and sovereignty in all things.

It is reasonable to fall to my knees and worship the God who holds all things together by the power of his might and to release to him all that I am and all that I have.

It is reasonable. It is not always easy.

Many years ago, when I was a young mother, I experienced a time of deep discouragement and confusion. My children were babies—an infant and a toddler—and the infant was sick most of the time. My husband's job required long hours and a heavy travel schedule, so I had no help, no relief during lonely days and long, sleepless nights. I had one urgent prayer during that time: "Please let the baby sleep tonight." Sometimes I varied it slightly: "Could she please take a nap today, just a short one?"

Most of the time, God answered, "No," punctuated with a baby's high-pierced squeal.

One day, after yet another sleepless night and an emergency trip to the doctor, I poured out my discouragement to my dad, who had come to town for a short visit. He listened, sipped his coffee, then responded in his slow, quiet way. "Wouldn't it be great," he said, "if we could just walk through these experiences without ever getting upset or discouraged? If we could just accept that God is in control, that his good will is at work in the situation, and not let ourselves give in to anxiety and distress?"

I remember feeling angry. I argued that we are humans. Distress and anxiety and exhaustion are part of our experience. "Does God want us to deny our humanity?"

"But would we be denying our humanity if we accepted our pain with a quiet, trusting heart? Doesn't God's presence in our lives and the knowledge of the truth give us the option of saying, 'Yes, this hurts, but God is doing something I don't understand, and I can trust him with it'? Do we have to agonize and whine?"

I wanted to whine. "Would it be so hard for God to make a baby take a nap, for Pete's sake? I mean, what high and holy purpose is being accomplished here?" I argued. "He spoke the world into existence. He could just blink and make this baby sleep through the night. Why won't he, just once?"

I'm older now, a little wiser, and I've had larger, more significant crises than sick and wakeful babies. I've learned through experience and observations that most of the time, God does not change our circumstances in response to our begging. He doesn't offer explanations for divorces, deaths, or frightening medical reports. He doesn't issue detailed, written reasons for our losses: financial, personal, or professional.

In his great book *Reaching for the Invisible God*, Philip Yancey wrote, "Perhaps we should say 'Christ is the pattern' rather than 'Christ is the answer,' because Jesus' own life did not offer the answers most people are looking for. Not once did He use supernatural powers to improve His family, protect Himself from harm, or increase His comfort and wealth."[7]

God is still doing, and *not* doing, things I don't understand. He continues to allow me to be confused. He continues to withhold explanations. He continues to call me to submission to his sovereignty and an attitude of humility in response to his dealings with me. He continues to be, well, *God*.

What does all this mean to the serious disciple who wants to walk in steady obedience and grow in intimacy with God? It means, first of all, that we cannot truly enter the Master/disciple experience until we accept God's authority and sovereignty in all things.

Recognizing God's Authority

My horseback riding experience provides a helpful metaphor here. At the equestrian club where I first began riding seriously, there was an old cowboy named Billy. Billy knew everything there was to know about horses and riding. He looked like a rumpled, over-the-hill rodeo groupie, but he trained hunters and jumpers, not barrel racers.

I always liked it when I found Billy leaning against the fence of the jump ring when I was working Tess. He would watch me and tell me exactly what I was doing wrong, or right. When questions about feed, tack, or riding technique came up anywhere at the equestrian club, the first and best answer was, "Ask Billy." And whatever Billy said to do, I did it.

Billy was the master, you see. The rest of us were his disciples. We didn't question Billy if he said to sit back a little in the saddle, or tighten our legs, or drop our heels. Or use different reins, or a thicker snaffle bit. We didn't argue if he said to move our hands up two inches higher on the horse's crest.

Billy knew horses. He knew the sport of equitation. He knew the challenges of a cross-country course. He knew dressage. To dispute him showed arrogance, disrespect. It demeaned his reputation as a master of the sport. It demonstrated the rider's ignorance.

Many times, Billy shouted instructions to me that I didn't fully understand, but I believed he knew what he was doing. I made the subtle adjustments that at times felt awkward. With practice, the adjustments began to feel more natural.

Of course, when speaking of the nature of God, any human comparison will be inadequate. But let Billy's relationship with the riders at the Willow Bend Equestrian Club be a parable to help us better understand this truth: God is the Master. He knows the ways of the universe. He knows me; he knows my "way of going."

David said it well:

Lord. You know me, inside and out.
You have investigated me thoroughly, and I am
Completely known by you, in every nook and crevice
of my being.
You know every move I make—sitting, standing,
whatever I'm doing, you're aware of it.
From your throne in the heavens,
You read my thoughts. You always know
what I'm thinking, even when I don't know myself.
You know where I'm going, and where I've been.
You know all about me.
You're well acquainted with my way of going.
Nothing catches you by surprise.
Even before I speak, you know what I'm going to say.
Nothing about me is hidden from you.[8]

The thought of being known so intimately, to be so exposed, would be terrifying to us if we didn't have this confidence to lay alongside it: *God is good.* His character is distinguished by this: that his mercies are tender ones.[9] This is the rich, sweet morsel of truth ensconced in the theology of God's sovereignty and supremacy.

Charles Bridges, an obscure British preacher from the nineteenth century, wrote, "All the names of God are comprehended in this one of *Good*. God is good by nature, and His nature is not without activity."[10]

God's every action toward us flows from his goodness. Knowing this, we can safely humble ourselves before his sovereignty and confidently submit to his dealings with us.

Consider the Alternative

The alternative to submission and humility to God is always arrogance and pride. And where arrogance and pride are alive and active, no true discipleship can develop. No intimacy with God, no friendship, and no increasing levels of trust can grow.

Without submission and humility, the exercise of the other disciplines—prayer, worship, simplicity, sacrifice, fasting, chastity, celebration, service, and the rest—will be nothing more than chores performed in the spirit of the Pharisees. They will be wearying tasks yielding nothing but futility and disappointment, or a delusional sense of power and grandeur.

Not Restricted to the Heavenly Realm

If it is difficult to humble ourselves before God our Creator and submit to his dealings with us, how much more difficult it is to be humble and submissive toward our fellow creatures. And yet Scripture teaches us that these disciplines are not restricted to the heavenly realm. Paul the Apostle wrote clearly, "Submit to one another out of reverence for Christ."[11]

Whole books about submission exist, usually written to women, specifically about marriage. A major Protestant denomination devoted a week of sessions at a recent annual convention to figuring out how to articulate and publish its position on how and when women must submit to their husbands.

We cannot escape the principle of submission in marriage. It is complex, especially in very troubled marriages where one spouse is not a believer or is an immature, troubled believer; or in marriages where injury and abuse are commonplace. But often, folks take passages out of context and apply them unwisely. In desperate situations people would be better served by heeding the verse from Proverbs that says, "Leave the presence of a fool, / Or you will not discern words of knowledge."[12]

I believe in biblical submission in marriage. I love God's plan for leadership in the home. But it troubles me that more Christians aren't taught *mutual submission* as a spiritual discipline that is required of all who call themselves Jesus' disciples.

While differing factions argue and discuss the dynamics of submission in marriage, Paul's command addressed all believers. Richard Foster wrote:

> It is a posture obligatory upon all Christians: men as well as women, fathers as well as children, masters as well as slaves. We are commanded to live a life of submission because Jesus lived a life of submission, not because we are in a particular place or station in life. Self-denial is a posture fitting for all those who follow the crucified Lord.[13]

We are to submit to one another. Foster also said, "The touchstone for the biblical understanding of submission is Jesus' astonishing statement, 'If any man would come after me, let him deny himself and take up his cross and follow me' (Mark 8:34)."[14]

We do not study or pursue the discipline of submission simply for the sake of learning when to give in or to whom we should humble ourselves. We exercise submission in order to pursue Christ, to be like him, to express the reality of kingdom life in this world. And through submission to one another we learn to recognize the sufficiency of God. When we relinquish our "rights" to our own way, God makes himself known to us in ways we never imagined possible.

Reverence for Christ fuels the discipline of submission. As we submit to his authority, we are better able to submit to others, allowing them to be the persons God created them to be; acquiescing to their needs and choosing to meet them while trusting the transcendent, sovereign God to meet our own.

The Attitude of Christ

The discipline of submission seems to travel best in the company of humility. Concerning humility, there is no better word than this:

> Your attitude should be the same as that
> of Christ Jesus:
>
> Who, being in very nature God,
> did not consider equality with God
> something to be grasped,
> but made himself nothing,
> taking the very nature of a servant.[15]

This is an astounding truth. God the Son did not grasp the glory that was due him; rather he made himself "nothing."

Is there anything more contrary to our culture than the idea
of being nothing?

Is there anything more contrary to our individual natures
than being a servant?

Yet this is the expression of humility. I think of it like this: I
don't insist on being first, or having the best, or having what I
want at the expense of what you want or need, because there is
nothing in me that makes me any more inherently deserving of it
than you. So, exercising humility, I'll let you have it.

The great irony of our faith is that Jesus Christ, by nature
fully God, was inherently deserving of all that was best and first.
Yet he willingly put it aside in order to serve his Father's purpose.

Every day of my life, opportunities exist for me to exercise
humility. Every day I can pass up claiming the best and the first
for myself. Every day I can reject the spirit of entitlement that
wars with humility. I can refuse to be demanding—of others, and
of God; I can refuse to insist that I deserve to have my expectations met, my dreams fulfilled, my life made easy and smooth.
And exercising humility, I can choose to release others from the
bondage of my expectations.

How subtle those expectations may be, yet how destructive.
How blinded we are to the truth about them: that they are evi-
dences of our arrogance, manifestations of our attitudes of entitlement—that we deserve something from others, such as their
attention, their time, their money, their respect. Often we
believe we deserve certain kinds of behavior from certain people
in our lives, that our position—in business, in the church, in our
family—makes us worthy. Expectations are never more dangerous than in the home. How true the maxim that "families can
become ghettos of unfulfilled expectations."[16]

Teresa of Avila wrote, "There is no danger so obvious as this concern about honor and whether we have been offended."[17]

Expressing humility, in the power of the Holy Spirit, we yield our hopes and dreams to God. In faith, we let go of our misguided, selfish demands—of others, of God, of ourselves. Recognizing the superior wisdom and love of God, we deliberately choose to stop fighting his loving, good will and stop demanding what we deem good treatment from others.

The result is freedom—our own! Freedom from the miserable, obsessive insistence that others meet or exceed our expectations and satisfy our hopes and dreams. Freedom from disappointment and disillusionment, for our only expectation is in Christ, and he has promised never to fail us. And freedom to love, unconditionally, as Jesus loves us.

Every day I can choose humility, acknowledging your great value to God—he died for you! I can recognize his sovereign right to direct your life and to gift you with blessings he withholds from me. I can acknowledge my own sinful nature that cost Christ his life and admit loudly, and often, "I am no better and no more deserving than anyone else on this planet!"

Knowing this, living as though this is true: this is the exercise of the discipline of humility. When it is exercised often, the muscles of the heart grow large and strong, able to sustain slights and offenses without erupting in fury and seeking retaliation. The ligaments of the spirit become agile, making it easier for us to bend over dirty feet and wash them.

Of all the disciplines, perhaps humility is the most beautiful. Imagine a family where each member is trying to secure the best for another!

Imagine living in community with people who truly understand biblical humility, people who are not so sensitive and self-conscious that they are injured by the slightest bump and rub. No worry and consternation haunt such a community, for "people who believe that nothing is owed to them never believe they are being mistreated."[18]

Imagine a church where people are falling over themselves trying to see that others' needs are met before their own!

You won't find pompous preening or attitudes of entitlement in a church where teaching includes humility as a spiritual discipline; nor will you find belligerence or abuse of power. You won't uncover these destructive characteristics in families in which both husband and wife teach and display humility either.

Fénelon wrote, "If we are convinced that nothing is our rightful due, then nothing will make us bitter."[19]

Humility at work in interpersonal relationships begins first in the throne room of the Almighty, where the creature has grasped the awesome truth of the Creator's worth and majesty. If it is found in families, local churches, businesses, leisure activities, and works of service and kindness, it is because men and women have practiced it in the quiet places of their hearts; it is because they have learned the two most important truths: that God is all and the creature is nothing.

What Submission and Humility Look Like

To many people, submission and humility suggest weakness—both of mind and of spirit. Two contemporary illustrations defy that image. Mother Teresa was by all accounts both humble and submissive to God. Who can forget the day she stood in the presence of the president of the United States, Bill Clinton, the leader of the free world, and called him to account for his stance on the dignity and sanctity of life?

In many instances, Mother Teresa faced the world's most

powerful leaders and spoke hard truths that contradicted the actions and policies of entire nations. An advocate for the weak, the poor, and the downtrodden, she boldly made their needs known. Without apology or embarrassment, she solicited help from the wealthy and called all people to live lives of greater compassion and service.

When Mother Teresa died, the world mourned her loss. Eternity will bear witness to the value of her life—a life characterized by deep love for Jesus and the disciplines of submission and humility.

But alongside the notable stands the noble, quiet example of "Angela" (not her real name). I know few people who have suffered as she has. Born into a generation that had little understanding of mental illness, Angela lived for more than forty years with severe nervous disorder. Christians often shamed her for being so fearful—having no faith—and strangers stared at her when an episode sent her running blindly, wild with unexplained terror.

Misdiagnosed, misunderstood, Angela was at one time taking high doses of antiseizure medication for what doctors thought was epilepsy. But nothing worked. Finally, desperate, Angela flushed all the medications she was taking and threw herself into the arms of God, begging for healing, for some kind of relief.

"I remember kneeling on the floor beside my bed and giving everything to God—my husband, my children, my life. I literally gave him my breathing, eating, surviving. I prayed, 'If I am dying, and this is the end of my life, I choose to live it in you and trust you with my illness.'

"I consciously said the words, 'If he slays me, I'll still worship him.'"

God spared Angela's life, although stopping the drugs cold turkey could have killed her. Healing didn't come quickly. It would be several more years before a wise and sensitive doctor would correctly diagnose Angela with severe panic disorder, an illness that appropriate medication now controls.

"So much of my life seemed to be surviving and living on the edge of great anxiety, yet God alone never let me get to that lowest of places where I really wanted to die to escape the black hole. He alone has been my life. Only if he desires it will I ever know why, except that the Psalms say that trouble comes to man as sparks fly upward. He is Lord, even of the troubled times, and he is faithful."

Angela's words ring with strength made tensile by the exercise of humility and submission.

Relating to God through Humility and Submission

The purpose of every spiritual discipline is to train us to relate to God, to abide in him, and to discover his sufficiency in all things.

Humility trains us to recognize God's supremacy, to view ourselves as his creatures, to see him as the Potter, ourselves as clay. It trains us to acknowledge his greatness, his omnipotence, his transcendent nature, and to accept the reality of divine mystery in our lives. It trains us to deal gently with others, knowing that they too are made of "crumbly stuff,"[20] and not one of us is to be valued above the other.

The discipline of submission puts us in the position in which we can be trained, taught. It develops strong muscles for bending and washing feet and carrying crosses.

These are hard lessons. Humility and submission require us to let go of our idea of how life should be. They require us to relinquish our plans and expectations and let God arrange events and relationships according to his plan.

Shortly after my son's divorce, I realized that I had drawn a blueprint for my life that included plans for each member of my family. I loved that blueprint and protected it fiercely. When the flames of reality consumed it, I was devastated. After crying gallons of bitter tears and praying for many hours, I knew I had to submit to the sovereignty of God. I had to accept his right as my Creator to do whatever he wills with me, even if it included allowing this crushing heartbreak. It was a deliberate, albeit painful, act of humility to get on my knees and accept his sovereignty in that awful situation.

I recognized the fact that God is not obligated to explain himself to me. I acknowledged that much of my anger and frustration with God had to do with arrogance. I wouldn't have voiced it at the time, but my attitude was saying, "How dare you let this happen to my family!"

I had to concede, finally, that I was not intrinsically better than another. There is no reason why tragedy should touch other families and not mine.

As a visual demonstration of the exercise of submission and humility, and a statement of trust in God's goodness, I took a piece of notebook paper from my journal and at the top of the page I wrote the words: *My Agenda.*

Under that heading, I listed all of the dreams and wishes (expectations) I harbored for myself and for the ones I loved. Then I stood over a trash can and tore the paper into a hundred tiny pieces.

For months, I made this a daily exercise, dropping fluttering scraps of paper into my office trash can. I prayed for increasing faith to trust God with the rest of my life, and the lives of the ones I loved.

It's not a daily thing anymore, but occasionally I need that exercise of humility and submission. I have to write down my "plans" and then tear them up to remind myself clearly: God is sovereign and in complete control. He is the Creator, and I am the creature. With that reminder comes the assurance that, while his doings are often beyond my understanding, the volume of his love for me is beyond all measuring.

I remember these things when I whisper that one-word prayer, "*Asholdah*." Submission and humility are summed up in its utterance.

3

~

BROODING ON THE SCRIPTURE

THE DISCIPLINE OF STUDY

*T*he romance was limping along when the young lady confided to me, "He says he loves me, but he never really tries to get to know me. He has this idea of what I should be like—what he wants me to be like—but he never tries to discover who I really am. There are whole parts of me that he doesn't even know exist."

I don't have to tell you that soon after that conversation, the relationship died a painful death.

No human relationship can survive, or thrive, on fantasy. Nor can our spiritual relationship with God.

A. W. Tozer wrote, "Do not try to imagine God or you will have an imaginary God. . . . Brood on the Scripture and let faith show you God as He is revealed there."[1]

The discipline of study takes us into the Scripture where we can "brood," or mull over the truth and, by faith, discover God as he really is.

Knowing God

Ophelia Spradling Hughes was a woman who knew God. One of nine children born to a cotton farmer in Texas, she was ahead of her time. In 1926, she held degrees in biology, French, and music. She brought a passionate love of discovery to her study of the Bible.

In the early years of her marriage she gave birth first to two stillborn infants, then to a severely disabled son. Doctors advised her not to have any more children. The chances of having a healthy child were small, they said, and it was likely another pregnancy would kill her. When she discovered she was pregnant for the fourth time, she was terrified.

Finally one night, after hours of tearful praying, Ophelia lay in her bed and began reciting all she knew to be true of God. She reviewed his goodness, his power, his love, his great strength and sufficiency. This was the God she had found in the Bible. This was the God she could trust with her life and with this pregnancy. She released her fears to the Lord and determined to trust him utterly, regardless of the outcome of the pregnancy.

Six and a half months later, she gave birth to a tiny baby girl, and both mother and daughter survived and thrived.

I first met Ophelia when she was in her eighties. She was visiting her daughter, Johnnie, my friend and neighbor whose coffeepot is always full of fresh, hot Starbucks brew and whose heart is always full of welcome. Sitting there in Johnnie's kitchen, I remember sensing Ophelia's quiet strength and kindness. Humor shimmered on her face, and while I don't remember all that we talked about, I remember being keenly aware of God's presence. I was sorry when it was time to leave.

"Her calm, my calm," Johnnie once said, describing her mother. "Her peace, my peace."

What a legacy! To be known as a woman who experiences God as he truly is and trusts him fully with the deepest, most intimate details of her life. To be a woman so confident of God's goodness and strength that calmness and peace radiate from her, warming the cold places in all who stand near her—I want to be such a woman. And I know that for this to be true of me, as it was of Ophelia, the discipline of study is essential.

I must get to know God—not a fantasy God, but God as he has revealed himself in the Bible.

Through Stories

In his great book *The Journey of Desire*, John Eldredge wrote:

> I could tell you a few facts about God. . . . He is omniscient, omnipotent, and immutable. There—don't you feel closer to Him? All our statements about God forget that He is a person, and as Tozer says, "In the deep of His mighty nature He thinks, wills, enjoys, feels, loves, desires, and suffers as any other person may." How do you get to know a person? Through stories. All the wild and sad and courageous tales that we tell—they are what reveal us to others. We must return to the Scriptures for the story that it is and stop approaching it as if it is an encyclopedia, looking for "tips and techniques."[2]

Reading that, I thought of my friend Carolyn. I could describe her to you as witty and entertaining, and you might get a vague idea of a pleasant person. But if I tell you the story of how I first met her, well, let the story speak for itself.

It was twenty years ago. We were sitting on bleachers watching our sons lose a soccer game on a muddy field in Dallas. The score was five to one when the coach called time-out. I leaned forward to listen to his instructions to the dejected mob of muddy fifth-graders when a tiny, blond lady scooted close to where the team had gathered on the bench and whispered loudly, "Don't worry, boys, we've got 'em right where we want 'em!"

A surprised grin etched itself on my son's face. He poked an elbow into his buddy's ribs, laughed, and returned to the field ready to play again. I don't remember the final score that day, but it doesn't matter. The boys were winners, and they knew it. And I had a new best friend—a woman whose extraordinary, capricious, outrageous good humor could never be communicated by mere adjectives strung in a sterile narrative.

The point is this: the Bible is the story of God. It is filled with adventures, disasters, drama—all for the purpose of illustrating the character, the personality of this God who calls us into relationship with him.

The First, Best Story

Woven through the myriad stories of the Bible, pulsing through the hundreds of chapters, winding through the colorful variety of characters, and climbing through changing geographic scenes is the powerful theme of romance. It is a romance made wondrous and adventurous by rescue and redemption.

From beginning to end, one primary hero dominates the story. A powerful, dramatic plot reverberates throughout the pages, giving purpose and relevance to every smaller subplot; and a grand, climactic conclusion bursts forth in the final phrases of the text.

While I knew this about the Bible, I didn't quite comprehend the majestic significance of it until I started teaching a series of writing classes based on a book called *The Writer's Journey* (Michael Wise Productions, 1992). This book's premise is that an ageless structure exists in every enduring story. Many instructors consider *The Writer's Journey* essential reading for novelists and screenwriters because it teaches the elements that every story well told must include.

Christopher Vogler, the author of *The Writer's Journey*, based his premise on an older work, *The Hero with a Thousand Faces* by Joseph Campbell. Both writers contend that a good story will always have certain archetypes, certain plot points, a recognizable story structure. Going back centuries, even millennia, the authors identified these common elements in the oldest known stories. They found them in stories saved through oral history, in hieroglyphs drawn on cave walls, in narratives preserved on papyrus and stone tablets, and in stories set to print on the first printing presses. Today they are found in the most contemporary stories processed in Microsoft Word, or reduced to the format of a screenplay. Every enduring story will have these common elements identified by Campbell and Vogler.

As I studied and prepared my workshops for writers, I began recognizing Vogler's story structure in my Bible reading. The basic elements appear in Genesis; the story climbs and curves through the golden age of Israel, through her exile and captivity, and through the prophets. The plot introduced in Genesis continues through the Gospels, explained and extrapolated in Acts and the letters to the churches. Then in Revelation comes the finale, the grand conclusion that presents the prize, the ultimate victory.

I was overwhelmed as I considered the magnitude of all this. Because God is the originator of all things, the first and best Creator, because he is the Alpha and Omega, *his is the first story.*

It is the prototype for all other stories ever told and preserved.

How could it be otherwise? In the beginning was the Word. The Bible tells the oldest story, the first story ever given to human ears and hearts. From it, all other enduring stories draw their structure.

Within the Bible lies the pattern for every hero, every anti-hero, every lover, every loser, every mentor, every villain, every warrior, every jester. It is the source from which all other stories draw their dramatic elements, their concept of heroism, and the idea of romance—of love and love thwarted, and love consummated. It is an eternally unfolding story in which we are living, breathing characters.

God, the Ultimate Romantic

Authored by the Alpha and Omega, the Bible tells the story of beginnings and endings, and new beginnings. It is the story of time; it is the story of timelessness. It tells the story of a supreme, divine perfect being who calls himself "I Am," someone who is, at heart, the ultimate romantic.

If you study the Bible from beginning to end, you see God as a Lover whose sole intent is to win for himself a companion who is like him, and yet unlike him. It is the same in every true romance. A woman seeks one who is like her, yet different in gender. God seeks us, who are like him, made in his image, and yet unlike him, as we are finite, rather than infinite.

Within those parameters, he seeks a lover to share his glory and enter into his love. The narrative from Genesis to Revelation pulses with the intensity of God's passion for those who will accept his love and love him in return.

If you miss that theme in the Bible, you are reading a sterile narrative made drudgery by a litany of do's and don'ts. You are reading data, facts, of which "we have millions . . . all quite dead."[3] But if you keep the theme in mind, the narrative throbs with life!

As you read, you discover the compelling story of Jesus Christ, our King of kings, the Hero for all ages. His quest: to establish a kingdom in a land overridden and dominated by an evil warlord; to enter that enemy territory, defeat the wicked usurper, and claim for himself a bride who will share his victory and rule with him in love and beauty in a new, unblemished land.

As I consider the implications of all this, I feel excitement. Picking up my Bible to read, awe overtakes me. Because this grand story includes me in the plot.

I am the bride.

The Truth of It

How differently I read the Bible when I see that I am in it—I am part of the story from which all other stories derive their shape and structure. This God we often treat in such a casual, offhand manner, to whom we give an occasional nod as we browse a psalm or a proverb for the day—this God has given us the first and best love story. It is an adventure teeming with the most powerful and universal theme: romance. And I play a significant part in the plotline.

Through the discipline of study I immerse myself in the story—a story that is not fiction, but truth. Scores of books have been written to present evidence of the Bible's authenticity and its inerrancy, and it is important and exciting to study these. It is an amazing thing to see how God has preserved his story through the centuries.

As a writer and one who teaches those who want to write, I know how hard it is to make a story work: to identify a single theme and make it resonate throughout; to develop a plot and characters that are consistent from beginning to end. But God, infinite in his creativity and perfect in all his doings, has given us a volume that consists of sixty-six books, written by individuals separated by time, culture, geography, status, and education. Throughout this volume every aspect of the story agrees in theme and every line complements the other without contradiction.

The astounding story of the preservation of the Scriptures and the process of establishing the canon is itself a miracle; it is faith-building. In the end, we can only stand in awe of this great gift that God has given us, and praise him for his preservation and protection of it, and for the power it has to change us.

The documents stand as truth. The grandeur and nobility of the message make it transcend all other stories, all other writings. The Holy Spirit reassures us. The prophecies fulfilled in Jesus Christ demand our belief. The resurrection and ascension of our crucified Savior, witnessed by hundreds, declare the closing arguments for the validity and truth of God's Word.

We can read it with confidence, knowing God is the Author; that he has spoken. I can hear his story and participate in its unfolding through the discipline of study.

Read Anyway

So here lies this black leather book, or red, or navy blue. And in it lies a story so grand we are amazed. To think that a majestic, all-powerful being is loving beyond our comprehension, and that his dearest delight, that for which he sacrificed his only Son, is to be in a relationship with us. That he loves us and wants to spend the aeons of eternity sharing his glory and the magnificent wonders of creation with us—this is more than we could have ever wished for or imagined.

Our hands touch the leather, open the cover, but so often our minds rush off in a dozen different directions. Our thoughts skitter like marbles on a tabletop. To-do lists pull at our attention. E-mail and blinking answering machines beckon us. Family chores, career obligations, friends, and relationship issues all vie for our attention and our time. And even if we've carved out a few minutes in which to read and study, often the glory and transcendence of the message evade us. What's a disciple to do?

Read anyway.

Discipleship means doing things that may at first feel awkward—they are actions that someone else has modeled for us. Until we make them our own, through deliberate, consistent practice, they may not feel comfortable or even desirable.

Let me hark back to the riding analogy of earlier chapters. When old Billy the cowboy told me to push my heels down in the stirrups in order to ride better and have more leg control, it felt awful. I believed him when he said it would improve my riding—Billy knew about these things—but my legs rebelled. My calves ached for weeks as my muscles adjusted to the stretch.

In time, though, because I persevered and practiced the way Billy showed me, I grew accustomed to the position. I could feel how my balance and control improved, and even though it was a deliberate decision to push my heels down every time I rode, it became easier and easier. And on those days when my legs were tired, or when I was distracted, I pushed my heels down anyway, because I had learned that I could ride better that way.

How silly I would have been to refuse to do what Billy told me because it just didn't "feel right."

The metaphor is clear. I know that studying my Bible is important, whether I feel like it or not. The apostle Paul told me that the Bible profits me in every way. David the psalmist said the Bible is a light and a lamp—it illumines my way. Other passages extol the nature of God and give me reasons to trust, to hope; to keep on trusting and hoping. The prophets tell me what to look forward to. The Gospels show me God in flesh, Jesus. The letters to the churches teach me how to live my life, how to relate to others, how to serve God, how to love and pray and function in society.

And yet, many times it feels awkward to sit and read. It feels uncomfortable, forced. It is the same with any one of the disciplines, when we first begin exercising it. They may at first make us feel as if our spiritual muscles are being strained and pulled out of shape. But they are necessary if we are going to follow Jesus and experience intimacy with him. None is more necessary than study.

Our Master, the one whose disciples we claim to be, consistently demonstrated the value he placed on Scripture. The New Testament shows us a Savior who quoted the prophets, the poets, and the Law. He knew and understood the stories of Moses, David, Daniel, Jonah, and the other familiar characters of our faith. Often in his messages he alluded to them, drawing great significance from their experiences. He taught the Old Testament with authority that staggered the most learned rabbis of his time. Even as a youngster, Jesus displayed a passion for Scripture and his knowledge of it stunned the spiritual leaders of Israel.

Every sermon Jesus preached, every parable he taught, contained fruit sprouted from the seeds of Old Testament knowledge. He never spoke without the authority of Scripture. Even his prayers reflect knowledge of Scripture. And no wonder—he was the Word, in the beginning. And "without him was not anything made that was made!"[4]

It is an inescapable fact for those of us who want to do more than dabble in discipleship: study is essential. If Jesus, being fully God, valued the Scriptures during his sojourn in human flesh, can we do less?

The Decision to Study

I remember when study was for me a task riddled with all kinds of complications. I didn't fully understand how much God loved me, how he would love me whether I read my Bible or not. Like the Pharisees Jesus condemned, I lived according to rules and laws. Bible reading fell into the must-do category. It was not a joyful immersion into the heart of God, but rather a legalistic exercise. God would like me better if I read more, I thought. If I skipped a day, or a week, God would be displeased with me. Maybe he wouldn't even love me anymore.

The realization of God's deep, abiding, tender love for me has grown slowly, over long years of struggle. I yearn to live in the reality of that love every day, but it is a challenge for me. I do remember a time when the truth of his unconditional love for me began to penetrate my thinking, when I first began to grasp the truth of his heart: that I am his beloved, that he loves me *now*, no matter how I feel about myself, no matter how I act, no matter how I look. He loved me when he saved me, when I was his enemy, and he loves me now, and it has nothing to do with my performance or my Scripture reading schedule. It occurred to me that, in fact, if I never again opened a Bible, God would not stop loving me. He had never measured my value against my study habits, and he wasn't going to start now.

As I began to seek to live in the reality of God's unconditional love for me, I felt myself drawn to his Word. I wanted to read and study, because it was there in his message to me that I found the greatest acceptance, the greatest love I had ever known.

It was there that I encountered God. I discovered the "sacramental quality" of the Word of God, that reading it "makes God present not only as an intimate personal presence, but also as a presence that gives us a place in the great story of salvation."[5]

There are times when I don't want to sit and study simply because other activities are more enticing. But that is when the word *discipline* becomes relevant. It is not discipline enforced because I think God will stop loving me, or because I fear disappointing a watching Christian community that imposes its expectations on me. Unlike earlier years, when I read out of guilt, or because of legalistic obligations, I now read even when I might not feel like it because I know God will meet me in his Word, and because I want his imprint on my heart.

There is another category of reluctant Bible students. My husband falls into this group. Study is hard for him—he's dyslexic. Reading is work that can bring beads of sweat to his forehead, but by sheer determination he has mastered techniques for navigating Scripture. He teaches an adult Sunday school class and spends many hours a week reading not only his Bible, but a couple of commentaries with which he has become comfortable. But his greatest aids in the discipline of study have been books and sermons and seminars on tapes and CDs. He has been able to enjoy great Christian writers and teachers as well as Scripture spoken on tape.

Ken and I have learned to appreciate each other's different study habits. He gives me grace for being somewhat obsessive—I collect index cards with quotes from favorite authors, along with pages of handwritten notes filed in neon-colored folders. And I've learned the best places to shop for books on tape. I'm in awe of the audiographic memory God gave Ken to compensate for his dyslexia. He's never forgotten anything he ever heard! (This is a good thing for a Bible student, not necessarily for a husband.)

Along with others who share our pilgrimage, we're convinced of two things about the discipline of study: First, it is essential for growth and intimacy with God. Second, it will not make God love us more, or increase our value to him. He already gave everything he had to redeem us. We are precious to him whether we ever read a word in his Book or not.

If the two statements seem opposed, it is because the heart of the matter is grace, and grace always sets up a tension in the discussion of human life and habits. On the one hand, our natural mind-set tells us that we must perform in order to have value. Yet the Bible teaches us that God's love already enveloped us while we were his enemies. Study doesn't increase his love for us. It can, however, increase our love for him and enable us to travel this life with peace and wisdom.

Study in Context

Paul wrote, "Through the Word we are put together and shaped up for the tasks God has for us."[6] It is through the *whole* Word that we are "shaped up," not just the portions that are comfortable and agreeable to us. We can't apply only the verses and concepts that we like. We can't gain all that God wants us to gain through study if we pick and choose certain pieces of Scripture, like tools, for "fixing" ourselves. We need the whole of it if we are going to know God as he really is, if we are going to learn to live in the reality of his kingdom. Context is essential.

A recent conversation with my friend Carolyn illustrates this. If you had overheard us chatting over coffee at our favorite French bakery, you would have heard several references to Carolyn's mother, who suffered a stroke a few months ago. If you had walked away for only a moment, you might have missed our transition from the topic of ailing parents to the discussion of dangerous family pets, and if you came back to hear us discussing methods of euthanasia, you would have been appalled.

How often do we experience similar confusion when we enter God's story without taking time to discover the context, without noticing the transitions in the conversation. God's Word, his story, is his conversation with us! It matters where we come into it.

In our hurried lives, we too often open our Bibles and pick a verse or two and read without any sense of context. We miss the great significance of one passage while completely misconstruing the meaning of another. It happens all the time. Disciples grab at a verse for comfort or instruction, never taking the time to look at the verses that come before and after it.

My mother-in-law has for years fussed about preachers and teachers who read, "No eye has seen, / no ear has heard, / no mind has conceived / what God has prepared for those who love him" and then stop. "Read the next verse!" my mother-in-law almost shouts. "See? It says, 'But God has revealed it to us by his Spirit'!"[7]

Stopping short of verse 10 means missing out on a magnificent truth: God, through his Holy Spirit and through specific passages of Scripture, has revealed to us his glory and his secret wisdom. Because of that revelation, we can live joyfully. We can celebrate the kingdom of God now, with confidence in his coming reign, with excitement for the glory that will be revealed for us to see with physical eyes.

When we read hurriedly, without taking time to examine the context, we miss out on the fullness of the Bible's message. We miss out on the beauty that can fill our souls and satisfy our yearning for transcendence.

Open the Book

A friend has been gently sharing her faith with a business associate. Recently the associate blurted, "I'm going to read through the Bible, starting in Genesis." My friend was a little worried about this.

"What's going to happen when she gets to the place in Genesis where Cain marries? Whom did he marry? I can't wait for her to ask me that one."

Make no mistake. Some parts of the Bible are difficult to understand. Jumping in at Genesis with no prior knowledge of God and the truth may be a bit daunting. Most Bible teachers I know recommend starting in the Gospels. There we see Jesus, God in the flesh, and we can begin to get a glimpse of the Father through the Son.

Study aids abound. I recently bought a study Bible that tags key words in the text and then gives the original Greek, Aramaic, and Hebrew definitions. Simple, timeworn passages gain new power for me as I discover the imagery in certain words. For example, the Psalms are full of the word *keep*, as in "He will keep thy foot from stumbling" and "He will keep thee from harm." Turning a few pages to the Hebrew lexicon in the back of the study Bible, I discovered that the word we have translated "keep" describes the way a gardener tends his garden—wisely, gently, and with knowledge of all that the coming season will bring. A treasure!

I enjoy reading works that show that the Bible is an adventure and I am a participant in it. John Bunyan's *The Pilgrim's Progress* helps me visualize the reality of the spiritual truths of Scripture. *Hinds' Feet on High Places*, by Hannah Hurnard, is another allegory that takes me into the invisible realities of faith. (Find them on tape, if you need to.)

Devotional books, such as Oswald Chambers's *My Utmost for His Highest*, Eugene Peterson's *Living the Message*, and Amy Carmichael's *Edges of His Ways*, give me a starting place for focusing my thoughts on God and lead me into quietness before I study.

Books about the Bible are no substitute for reading the Bible itself, but many Christian books have led me into fresh understanding of Scripture passages whose meaning eluded me before. For that reason, I keep both volumes of John Piper's *A Godward Life* alongside my chair with my Bible. I keep Henri Nouwen's works close by, as well as books by George MacDonald and Teresa of Avila, and others that, in a brief chapter, can explain and illustrate biblical principles that awaken change in me and stir me to greater love for God.

Recording the Journey

Years ago my mother suggested I buy a notebook about the same size as my Bible and keep it nearby when I study. Over the years I've filled several notebooks as I've written down how I've come to understand and apply a certain verse I've been studying.

There have been days when all I read was my notebook, not my Bible, but I was studying God's words all the same. I was reading verses I had copied down, reviewing the meaning God had made clear to me. Recently I spent several days reading back through pages that traced my study of Psalm 75. I had copied several verses and then asked myself questions, recorded answers, mulled over the thoughts triggered by the questions, and finally wrote this paraphrase of verse 2: "God chooses the occasions of our lives—the appointments, the special gatherings and the events—*where* we meet and *whom* we meet! His decisions and choices in these matters are *right* and *good.*"

If knowledge of God was the goal of study, I achieved it in that exercise. I went into the day knowing that God was in control of all that I would encounter that day, that nothing would surprise him. Whatever he chose for me would be for my good.

Over time, using this notebook method of study caused my confidence in God to surge. My faith has swelled with new expectations of his grace.

The point is not to be held to a rigid form of study because that's the way someone else does it. The point is not to read so many chapters or verses a day. God is not keeping count. The point is to discover and experience God through study. The point is to listen to God. The point is to immerse ourselves in the story that God has authored, and to enter into the adventure of eternal love and redemption that is unfolding.

Keep Turning the Pages

A few years ago my daughter, Molly, faced a terrible disappointment. I wanted to comfort her, to tell her everything would be fine, but the words sounded trite even to my ears. Her suffering was acute.

I prayed for her constantly and mulled over what I could say to her. She wanted something from me, expected something from me—*anything* that might relieve the pain she was feeling.

One afternoon, as we sat together and talked about what was

happening in her life, I said the only thing that kept coming to my mind. "Just keep turning the pages, honey," I said. "God has written this story, and it's not over yet. Don't give up. Turn the page and watch to see how this plot will unfold."

I was telling her, "Enter into the story. Don't just read words on a page. Crawl into the book, make it your story, by faith. Walk through the chapters with an eye on the story line and absolute confidence in the Author."

What a difference it makes to read the Bible with a sense of the whole in mind, to let yourself enter the adventure set in motion by God.

To those who make study a legalistic punishment, let me encourage you to spend some time visualizing the whole of the Bible—its theme that resonates with romance and rescue, redemption, and rejoicing. Do as Eugene Peterson suggested: "Bring the leisure and attentiveness of lovers to this text."[8]

John Piper encouraged us to "prayerfully ransack the Bible."[9] I love the image that conjures up: grabbing and shaking and pummeling the pages until the wealth of it, the majesty of it, tumbles out, filling us, overflowing and spilling out all around us, lighting our lives, delighting our souls.

Yet the serious disciple of Jesus cannot forget this warning: "Conceit of knowledge is the greatest enemy to knowledge, and the strongest proof of ignorance."[10] We must always remember that "the great end of all study—all theology—is a heart for God and a life of holiness."[11]

Hearing the Voice of God

Henri Nouwen wrote: "The full power of the word lies, not in how we apply it to our lives, after we have heard it, but in its transforming power that does its divine work as we listen. . . . It is in the listening that God becomes present and heals."[12]

Nothing is so vital to our lives than that we listen to the voice of God. That he, the great I am, would speak so that we can hear him—this is the most amazing thing! And what is it that we hear when we listen, through study? The psalmist said it best, I think: "One thing God has spoken, / two things have I heard: / that you, O God, are strong, / and that you, O Lord, are loving."[13]

Ophelia Hughes learned the truth of this. After Ophelia's death at age ninety, her daughter, Johnnie, found this message written on the back of an envelope tucked inside a kitchen cabinet: "I have unshakable faith in the perfect outcome of every situation in my life, for I know that God is in absolute control. For every crisis there is Christ."

The handwriting is shaky. At the time Ophelia wrote it, she had suffered a broken pelvis and was no longer able to live alone. The independence she had enjoyed as a brilliant, active woman was gone, and she was totally dependent on others for the most basic human needs. But the truth of God's love and strength never left her thoughts. Her faith in him was unshakable.

Martin Lloyd-Jones once said, "The measure of the strength of a man's faith always is ultimately the measure of his knowledge of God."

Study shows me this God, who sums up his message to me in two words: strength and love. This is the God of the Bible. In him we have everything we will ever need.

4

~

ASSEMBLING A LIFE BEFORE GOD

THE DISCIPLINES OF SIMPLICITY
AND SACRIFICE

I'll never forget watching my son, Matt, pack for college. He had emptied his closets and his dresser drawers, setting out piles of stuff he'd accumulated through nineteen years of living. Clothes draped a basketball hoop that hung on his bedroom door. His bed sagged beneath a pile of jackets, sports gear, and boxes filled with miscellaneous items of indeterminate value—to me, anyway.

"Hey, don't take that out!" Matt shouted as I tried to remove a strange-looking weaponlike thing. "That's my paintball gun! I'll need that! And that too!" He yanked a camouflage jacket out of my hands and stuffed it back into a box already overloaded.

"Son, you're going to college, not to boot camp," I argued. "If you've got time to play paintball, it would be better spent studying." I pulled a weird-shaped helmet/face-mask thing out of another box. "This stays," I said, stashing it in the hall closet along with the paintball gun.

We wrestled with Matt's stuff off and on for several days

before loading it into his Jeep and the family car trunk and back-seat. Finally it was time to head for the men's dorm at Texas Tech.

Two years later, we went through the same experience as we loaded our daughter, Molly, for the journey to college.

It has been several years since those times of sorting, packing, and pitching out in preparation for the journey into a new phase of life, but when I began studying the discipline of sacrifice, those memories flooded back. They seemed especially relevant as I read this quote from Eugene Peterson: "A sacrifice is the material means of assembling a life before God in order to let God work with it. Sacrifice isn't something we do for God, but simply setting out the stuff of life for him to do something with."[1]

I love the visualness of the phrase "setting out the stuff of life." It draws a picture of how I ought to present myself to God, inviting him to scrutinize my life, my lifestyle. It calls me to simplicity of purpose and the often painful work of letting go. It invites me to learn that "detachment is not loss—it is a precondition for fresh creativity."[2]

That concept eluded my children as teenagers entering college. It often eludes me as well. I love my "stuff." I don't want to let go of it.

Exercising sacrifice and simplicity is seldom painless. But discipleship requires it of us. It is essential if we are going to be anything more than fickle admirers of the Son of God.

Travel Light

When Jesus sent his disciples off on their first adventure in discipleship, these were his instructions: "Take nothing for the journey except a staff—no bread, no bag, no money in your belts. Wear sandals but not an extra tunic."[3]

After sending two kids off to college, I can appreciate Jesus'
intent here. He was sending *his* "kids" out into a growing-up experience. He knew what they would need, and what they wouldn't.

If I put myself in the company of those first disciples, a dozen
arguments come swiftly to mind. I imagine discomfort, inconve-
nience, austerity. But Jesus' instructions were very clear. They are
a powerful metaphor for today's disciples, offering us insight into
the exercise of simplicity and sacrifice—disciplines that train us
to rely on God, to experience his presence, to discover his passion for caring for us, and to enjoy his intimate companionship.

The Context of the Cross

We can't talk about simplicity and sacrifice without standing in
the shadow of the cross.

Every day, God continues to demonstrate the commitment
and love he displayed at Calvary when he sacrificed his Son to
buy us out of slavery to sin. His commitment to care for his people and to entrust them with his kingdom purposes hasn't weakened through the centuries. His sovereignty and his
omnipotence are still at work for us. His gentleness and compassion are "new every morning."[4]

In this context God calls us to simplicity and sacrifice in the
pursuit of greater knowledge of him. In this context, we must
take seriously the same command that Jesus' first followers heard
as they embarked on the adventure of discipleship.

Take No Bread

"Take no bread," Jesus instructed. Only a few days earlier, these
same disciples had heard Jesus say: "Do not worry about your life,

what you will eat or drink. . . . Is not life more important than food? . . . Look at the birds of the air; they do not sow or reap or store away in barns, and yet your heavenly Father feeds them. Are you not much more valuable than they?"[5]

It wasn't that Jesus wanted his disciples to be hungry. He wanted to feed them *himself*.

The principle of simple trust in God's promise to provide appears over and over again in both the Old and the New Testaments. God wants us to live simply in regard to the body's needs. His provision extends not to our stomachs only, but to all our physical needs. He wants us to live without bondage to fear for our physical life.

It's not easy. We live in dangerous times. As I write this, newscasts are filled with stories about anthrax spores traveling through the U.S. mail. Economic realities in the wake of September 11, 2001, have shut down companies, filled unemployment lines, and slashed stock prices that represent retirement income for many Americans. With every day come new reports of murderous threats, increased dangers in our homeland and around the world. Add to these the very personal concerns and dangers we face: my friend Kathy just endured surgery for skin cancer, and my friend John learned recently that he has Lou Gehrig's disease.

While I may not worry about where my next meal is coming from (although countless millions do), I do wonder about my physical safety. If bioterrorism is a reality, will sufficient vaccines and antibiotics be available for us, for our children?

If disease or catastrophe doesn't take my life, what will old age look like for me? Will our retirement plans be sufficient? Will death come before I am unable to care for myself?

George MacDonald wrote, "Because we easily imagine ourselves in want, we imagine God ready to forsake us."[6]

The news on the television and in the morning paper shouts at us, nearly drowning the still, small voice of God who whispers, "Don't worry about your life."

Can it be true?

Is it possible to live without worry about our physical bodies, what we will eat, how we will be cared for, how we will survive?

What does obedience to this command look like? Does it mean we are exempt from being prudent about our physical needs? Are we allowed to be careless and thoughtless?

Just the opposite is true.

Paul the Apostle taught that a Christian's body is the temple that houses the Holy Spirit. We are each handcrafted, formed and shaped by God himself who blew into us the breath of life. For us as disciples, the implication is profound: we look after the body in appropriate ways because it is God's creative handiwork, and it is the vehicle through which we live out our discipleship.

But we deliberately set aside a preoccupation with the body's needs, its safety, and its appetites. We deliberately choose to live simply because we take Jesus at his word. We believe him, that his Father cares, that our bodies matter to him, that he infused us with significance when he put his hand to the potter's wheel and formed us from the clay of the earth. We choose to trust God to be sufficient for our bodily needs, both now and in the future, in ways we can't foresee.

Uncluttered Lives

"Take no bread" is a command that offers me simplicity. It enables me to live an uncluttered life, unburdened by obsessive concerns for my physical self. It shows me how to sacrifice, how to give up my idea, or my culture's idea, of what is needed for physical security and satisfaction. It releases me from obsessive fears for my personal safety. It sets me free to give generously, sacrificially, to meet the bodily needs of others without fearing I will be bereft.

But perhaps more than anything, it reminds me that I am a spiritual being as well as physical. It reminds me that, no matter how safe I think I am, no matter how full my stomach and how secure my portfolio, unless the Bread of Life is nourishing me, I will never be anything but anxious and hungry. I will never be truly secure.

Take No Bag

To the original Twelve, Jesus' command to "take no bag" was specific, concrete. When obeyed, it gave the disciples opportunity to see the miraculous provision of their heavenly Father. For us today embarking on the adventure of discipleship, it's a metaphor that can teach us the liberty of sacrifice and simplicity.

God does not want us to depend on anything we can carry with us into this love relationship with him. He doesn't want us to derive security from our diplomas, our certificates of accomplishment, our trophies, our beauty supplies, or whatever paraphernalia might be in our "bag." Nor does he want us weighted down with emotional "baggage."

To the guilt-ridden child of God, still lugging around a bag heavy with stones of regret, Jesus says, "Drop it!"

To pompous, arrogant Christians, quick to open their bags and exhibit trophies of their accomplishments, Jesus says, "Don't! Put it down and leave it behind."

To all of us, he says, "Simplify your lives. Leave behind whatever distracts you from celebrating and rejoicing in the immensity of God's grace toward you."

Bags of All Kinds

A few years ago, I was standing in line to buy cookies at a mall when I noticed a teenage boy in front of me wearing a letter-man's jacket. It was obvious he was a very active and talented boy because his jacket was covered with patches, and the patches were covered with gold pins. It was also obvious he attended a Christian high school: one of his letters was for "soul winning."

You have to wonder who came up with this idea. How many school administrators sat in a tiny room and pondered before they decided to designate soul winning as letter-worthy? What scale did they use to determine the number of souls that had to be "won" in order to qualify for a letter? How many additional souls were necessary to get those little gold pins? Is soul winning a sport or an art, like theater or music?

We may laugh at the absurdity of a "letter" for soul winning, but most of us have to admit that it is tempting to flaunt our accomplishments. It is easy to be impressed with ourselves.

Jesus' command to "take no bag" meant the disciples shouldn't carry around souvenirs of their successes.

Lay Aside Every Weight

If I want to go forward into maturity in Christ and enjoy intimate friendship with God, I have to ask myself, *What am I carrying with me as tokens of my importance and value?*

It's not a one-time question. Daily, many times a day, I find myself tempted to draw meaning and significance from my accomplishments, or from my connections or small successes. I allow myself to rely on these things, as though they could actually infuse my life with the kind of dignity and confidence for which I so deeply yearn.

I design a fashionable bag for myself and drag it into conversations and relationships, hoping that the people I'm interacting with will perceive me as important, accomplished, worthy of admiration. And when the responses aren't what I seek, I plunge into self-consciousness and fear.

Worse yet, I drag my "bag" into God's presence and attempt to show him how great I am, how deserving I am of his love. Or I sit and agonize over the emptiness of my bag, over the failures and futile efforts of my life.

Jesus says, "Forget the bag! Sacrifice the things you carry with you—both the good and the bad. Simplify. Live in childlike trust in the God who forgave you and dressed you in the incomparable beauty of my righteousness. Let him crown you with his beauty and dignify your existence with his love and his kingdom purposes."

The writer of Hebrews 12 told us to "lay aside every weight." The message is clear: going forward in obedience means leaving behind the things that the world's philosophy insists are essential to our sense of significance.

This is a kind of sacrifice, for we are giving up the very things that have been life to us. But such sacrifice results in the greatest liberty imaginable: to experience all of Christ that God wants to make available to us in this life.

Paul the Apostle wrote, "One thing I do: Forgetting what is behind and straining toward what is ahead, I press on toward the goal to win the prize for which God has called me heavenward in Christ Jesus."[7]

When Paul laid his all at the foot of the cross, that included the debt of his guilt for persecuting Christians and attending their execution. It included the credit he might have been tempted to claim for being a "Jew among Jews," a keeper of the

Law, a zealous intellectual. When he entered the adventure of discipleship, Paul took with him only what God himself provided: grace and mercy in abundant measure.

Inadequate for God's Treasures

"Take no bag" means sacrificing the things that the world, or my culture or community, designates as essential to my sense of self, my sense of security and well-being. It means leaving behind everything I ever depended upon for value and significance, dropping the baggage that's heavy with the burdens of my failures and disappointments. Compared to the eternal gifts God wants to give me, these collections are mere trinkets, broken toys.

When we decide to leave these things behind, we make space in our lives for the gifts Jesus' death purchased for us: a royal identity, security beyond imagining, freedom from bondage to self and ego, forgiveness and release from the hauntings of guilt and failure.

No bag we could carry can accommodate such great treasures as these.

Take No Money

"Take no money," Jesus said.

We respond, "You must be kidding."

How does a disciple live in obedience to such a command? If we have wealth, do we give away all our assets, close out our bank accounts, and empty our pockets of all but keys and a comb? Even the poorest in our communities have some loose change—is Jesus demanding that they give away even that small amount?

A careful reading of the Bible, both the New and Old Testaments, convinces me that this is not a true and faithful understanding of God's intent. The Book of Proverbs is full of instructions on being prudent stewards, planning wisely for financial needs. New Testament writers taught first-century Christians to take care of the poor, and only individuals who had some money to share could provide such care.

Still, the command "take no money" lies there on the page, requiring our attention. What does it mean? How does this play out in our lives? What happens to us, in us, when we agree to obey this command?

Simplicity of Purpose

Eugene Peterson's words on sacrifice are helpful here. We must set out our financial resources, regardless of their size, and let God direct their use, being willing to sacrifice whatever he asks for. Such sacrifice, however, can come joyfully and fearlessly only from a heart that is characterized by simplicity of purpose.

So, what drives us as individuals in our use of money? If our primary purpose is the pursuit of ever-increasing knowledge and experience of God, then money will be nothing more to us than a tool for accomplishing his will and serving his kingdom. Out of love for him, we will place it on the altar willingly, cheerfully.

Scripture bears testimony to this. Money is a factor in discipleship only in the sense that we understand that however much we have, it belongs to God, not to us. We "take no money," except to take it to him.

Brother Lawrence wrote, "I have resolved to make the love of God the end of all my actions. I have been well satisfied with this single motive."[8]

If this "single motive" is uppermost in the minds of all disciples, it won't be a painful, heart-wrenching task to hand over our money to God. In fact, it will be a natural outflow of our devotion to him, the reasonable result of a passionate desire to see his purposes prevail instead of our own.

Rich and Poor Alike

Money concerns plague everyone, rich and poor alike. Greed and miserliness can take up residency in any heart. For all of us, being preoccupied with material things is "a flabby pursuit, offering nothing in our time of need."[9]

Jesus addressed every attitude toward money, from the smugness of the rich to the insecurities of the poor. His command reaches beyond first-century Christians and into the wallets of everyone who desires to be a true disciple. *All* disciples, regardless of financial condition, must respond to this common imperative: to live free from bondage to money: the obsessive pursuit of it, the fearful hoarding of it, the temptation to draw significance and power and security from it.

I confess that this is a difficult area for me. I grew up in a very modest family. Our lifestyle was simple, our resources limited. As a college student I had little more than pocket change, sometimes barely enough to buy panty hose after writing the check for my room and board each month. I worried about money all the time.

When I married Ken, I discovered that he seldom worried about it. In fact, he liked to give it away.

We weren't wealthy. We seldom had more than enough to pay our bills, but still Ken was quick to share cash. I was usually stressed, fearful. At times I tried to talk him out of it. His answer: "It's God's money, isn't it? It's our job to distribute it where it's needed."

I'm not talking about the weekly tithe common to most churches—I was okay with that. I was even all right with the amounts he wanted to give to building funds from time to time. But I often struggled with all the times Ken gave money that didn't land in an offering plate, when there was no tax deductible receipt: to people whose cars were kaput, whose computers had konked out, whose kids were in trouble, and whose medical bills were suddenly staggering.

Living with Ken has taught me the meaning of "take no money." He has allowed me to be a partner in learning that it really is better to give than to receive. Ken's attitude toward money has freed him to be generous in lending as well. Because he isn't afraid it will cost him, he is quick to loan tools, equipment, cars, computers. These too belong to God, he says. How can we withhold from another what God has so generously allowed us to use and enjoy?

The Illusion of Security

Ken helps me to remember that money provides no real guarantees. At best, it is an insulator, buying me distance from certain discomforts and inconveniences. It buys coats when freezing weather hits; it pays electric bills when the Texas heat soars over one hundred degrees. It repairs cars and pays school expenses and feeds hungry mouths. But no matter how much we have, or don't have, it cannot purchase the things that are eternal.

Money offers nothing more than the illusion of certain kinds of security.

Money is not a bartering tool for the safety of the body, nor of the soul.

Money cannot purchase the things that transcend seasons

and social trends. It can't buy forgiveness, or peace, or deep joy, or the promise of friendship with the eternal, faithful, tender-loving God. It can't buy the confidence of resurrection.

As I write these words, I'm aware of the comfort of my life. During a Texas summer, I sit in a comfortable chair, cooled by an air conditioner that lets me forget about the record heat wave outside. I take frequent breaks to grab snacks from a well-stocked kitchen. If I crave something that I don't have, I drive my well-maintained car to a corner grocery and open my wallet to buy whatever I think I want. While I'm not rich by the standard of many, I have more than most people in the world.

I struggle with the issue of wealth: how dare I speak of it when I sit in such relative luxury, insulated from so many discomforts by the fact that there is money in a bank account that bears my name? I'm haunted by Jesus' words, "Take no money."

I have to remind myself daily that, as a disciple who desires to really know my Lord and experience him, money must be a factor only in the sense that I turn it all over to him. Whether it's a lot, or a very small amount, it's not mine. The checkbook may have my name on it, but Jesus and I both know it's really his. If he wants the cash in the bank to be given to help an out-of-work friend make a mortgage payment, or to aid a struggling college student, or to help a widow with car repairs and medical bills, the dollars are Christ's to spend. They are not mine to hoard or to agonize over.

At the same time, if my bank book is near empty, as it has been many times, and Jesus wants to show me how he can provide dollars in amazing ways, who am I to argue with him?

A few years ago, Ken and I went through serious financial struggles after a business partner suffered a stroke. Many times we wondered how we were going to meet our obligations. And still,

Ken insisted upon giving money away. He gave to the church, to friends, to our children, and to others whose needs were urgent. Always gladly and without regret, he wrote out checks that I, in my fear, would have never written. And during those days I learned the truth of Dallas Willard's words: "The cautious faith that never saws off the limb on which it is sitting never learns that unattached limbs may find strange, unaccountable ways of not falling."[10]

Many times, God broke our fall.

On one occasion an unexpected royalty check arrived in time for us to pay a tuition bill. On another, a business deal negotiated years earlier suddenly, surprisingly, paid a commission that settled our debts and enabled us to meet our obligations.

Many times, it seemed as though "strange, unaccountable ways" held us up. Many times, Ken laughingly said, "God must be doing it with mirrors."

It was a scary time, an exhilarating time, and an important time. I learned that God would take care of me, that money doesn't provide security. *God* does.

Examining Our Values

Jesus' call to "take no money" challenges us to examine our values. "Do you value what I can give you more than the things you can buy with your money?" he asks. "Can you go forward into the adventure of discipleship without being in bondage to money—without being frantic as to whether you will have enough, or whether you will be allowed to spend it as you like?

"Will you walk away from your culture's attitudes about money? Attitudes formed by deeply ingrained fears, as well as attitudes of superiority and entitlement?

"Will you walk away from your habits of spending, or saving, or hoarding, or whatever habits oppose liberty in me and violate the generosity of my Spirit? Will you walk in simple faith, trusting God to be sufficient for your every need? Or will you rely on the illusion of security that money offers?"

This is what Jesus asked the disciples when he told them to "take no money." Today he asks it again: "Will you trust me to be sufficient?"

Will we pursue a simple goal, that of knowing God and enjoying his fellowship above all other pursuits? Will we let go of the world's ideas of financial security and live sacrificially, gladly "stepping into the darkened abyss in the faith and hope that God will bear us up"?[11]

Such simple faith places us in the company of mighty saints who delighted in being called "childlike people . . . foolish enough to trust God's wisdom and the supernatural equipment of God."[12]

Simplicity and sacrifice ask no less of us, nor offer anything less from God.

Take No Extra Tunic

The Greek lexicon says this extra garment was a decorative vest worn under the top tunic. "Leave it behind," Jesus said.

Once again, Jesus' command offers a metaphor for today's disciples who want to understand the disciplines of simplicity and sacrifice: God calls us to a life that is not preoccupied with physical appearance. He calls us to sacrifice any mind-set that relies on clothing, hairstyle, and body size, or any measure of physical beauty and ornamentation in order to feel significant and valuable. He calls us to a life that is free of bondage to physical appearance. He calls us to *unself*-conscious living.

Freedom from the Tyranny of Others' Opinions

When I moved to Dallas more than twenty years ago, I discovered that my idea of fashion was a bit out of sync. A local newspaper columnist added to my confusion when she wrote that, in Dallas, *casual* meant "minimum sequins." While I was still trying to adapt my wardrobe to this new information, the term *snappy casual* erupted in conversations. I was sure I didn't have anything that fit that category.

I confess that I am often vulnerable to others' ideas of what is attractive and fashionable. I don't want to wear bell-bottoms if capri pants are vogue. If "big hair" is out, I want "small hair." So Jesus' instruction to the disciples about not wearing a decorative vest under their tunics hits home with me.

It is always risky to begin a spiritual discussion about physical appearance; the potential for abuse and misunderstanding is huge. Do we really need another voice pronouncing judgment on how we look and what we wear? But Jesus' message is not one of judgment; it is one of freedom: freedom from the tyranny of others' opinions. Freedom from fear that we will not measure up to another's ideal of beauty, or fashion, or acceptable appearance.

Freedom from Vanity

It is also a message of freedom from vanity.

How hard it is to beat down pride when we have worked so hard to look a certain way to please a certain group, or simply to please ourselves. How quickly we can feel superior to those who haven't yet achieved our level of fashion panache. How easy it is for us to abuse those less well turned out, less "discriminating." How easy it is to be critical and unkind. How unlike the spirit of Christ, which teaches us to "take no extra tunic."

Gary Thomas condensed it into this: "The goal of simplicity is communion with God."[13] Such a goal is incompatible with a mind-set that is focused on acquiring more and better adornments in order to attract the attention of others.

Appropriate dress has a place in the life of every disciple. The apostle Paul told us that love does "not behave itself unseemly."[14] The original language suggests that when we are motivated and directed by love for God and for others, we will seek to behave appropriately in all circumstances.

It isn't a stretch to say that we will make appropriate decisions about our appearance. We won't wear grubby gardening clothes to the symphony if a clean outfit is hanging in our closet; we won't choose party attire for a funeral. But agony over how we look, over whether or not we will gain the approval of those we consider powerful and/or important to our sense of esteem—this has no place in our lives.

This issue will be more of a challenge to some of us than to others. But to all of us, Jesus says the same thing: "Don't be preoccupied with appearance, with clothing or fashion or body shape and size, to the point of bondage. Don't be so concerned about how you look that you are unable to focus your worship and adoration on the Creator who made you and promises to take care of you."

Notice the Lilies

"You worry too much about clothes," Jesus said in a sermon one day. "Haven't you noticed the lilies of the field? They don't labor or spin, yet they are adorned by beauty that even Solomon's greatest robes could never rival. It's your heavenly Father who clothes them."

Isn't it interesting that when Jesus pointed out beauty, it was for only one reason: to give credit to his Father? As I think about the clothes in my closet, and the beautiful things in the malls that beg for purchase, I have to scrutinize my heart. Does simplicity characterize me? Am I interested in one thing only: growing in communion with God and learning to enjoy him? Or am I in bondage to things that I think I need to make me presentable, acceptable, worthy of admiration?

God cares about the things that distract me from him, including unhealthy concerns about my appearance. He calls me to simplicity in the area of physical appearance. He calls me to sacrifice—to give up reliance on beauty and appearance as a source of significance. He calls me to discover his sufficiency, and to be preoccupied with his beauty and not worried about my own.

One day, not so very long ago, I was overcome by feelings of self-consciousness and inferiority. Uncomfortable in my surroundings, I felt my appearance was not holding up well in comparison to the beauty of the women around me. My emotions had barely reached the shape of conscious thought when the soft voice of the Lord whispered to my heart, "Jan, I can't take my eyes off you."

Suddenly, nothing else mattered. In Jesus' eyes, I was lovely. Feelings of inadequacy dropped away. All thought of comparisons faded. I couldn't stop smiling.

Only from Jesus can we receive the kind of unconditional love that will release us from the bondage of unreasonable physical standards of appearance and the strain of unfair comparisons. For some disciples-in-the-making, such freedom will require painful sacrifice. For others, it is an offer of relief and rest.

Wear Sandals and Carry a Staff

Many years ago I trekked down a remote region of the Grand Canyon to an ancient Havasupai Indian village located in its depths. The journey was arduous, but I was young, and I made it with energy to spare. I have to credit that to the advice of others who had made the hike before me, veterans who told me to wear good shoes and get a sturdy walking stick.

"Those are the essentials," they said. "Whatever else you take or don't take, be sure you have the basics." I think this is what Jesus was saying when he told his disciples to "wear sandals and carry a staff."

Don't forget the essentials.

Shepherd and Sovereign

Say "staff" and I think of the good Shepherd from David's psalm. I think of his promise to guide, protect, provide, and comfort. But held in the hands of the King of kings, the staff becomes a scepter representing sovereignty and the divine authority of our omnipotent God.

"Take it with you," Jesus tells us. We are to travel the path of discipleship gripping the staff as a symbol to remind us of the Shepherd's goodness and faithfulness, and as a symbol of his sovereignty and the strength he gladly exerts on our behalf to demonstrate his lavish love for us.

How much simpler (but not easier) would our trek be if we were conscious of the smooth, cool wood of the Shepherd's staff in our hands? How differently would we carry ourselves if it were the King's scepter we held so tightly, rather than our flimsy self-consciousness and our small, decaying trophies?

Ready for Anything

"Don't go barefoot," Jesus said to his disciples. Paul was more specific. He told us to have our feet "fitted with the readiness that comes from the gospel of peace.'"[15] Simply put, that means to be ready for anything.

Only the Christian who is confident in the goodness and sovereignty of God can do that.

Assured of the truth of the gospel—that God has made a way for us to become his children through trust in his Son, that we are his beloved, and that he has promised never to leave us or forsake us—we can be ready for anything that enters our lives.

What an amazing way to live! Confident, secure in the company of the Shepherd-King! Excited, alert, ready for anything we encounter, knowing that his strength will be sufficient. Simple? Yes. That's the point.

Relentless Tendency Toward Simplicity

Jesus is the ultimate example of the disciplines of simplicity and sacrifice.

> There is in the life and teachings of Jesus a relentless tendency toward simplicity . . . a steady impulse toward living at risk, with a kind of abandon to the Father's care that looks foolish to the well-off world. . . . There is a freedom *from* things and *for* the kingdom that thrills the heart of His disciples.[16]

Simplicity called from his heart, "Not my will but thine be done." Sacrifice cried out, "Into thy hands I commend my spirit."

Where to Begin

David the psalmist wrote, "I have declared my ways."[17] He laid out everything before God and said, "Here it is, Lord. You look it over."

This is where simplicity and sacrifice begin. We declare our ways. Like students readying for a life of adventure and growth, we pull out all that represents our lives to this point. Piece by piece, box by box, we set it before God—all the stuff we value and adore, our passions, our goals, our trophies. And then we stand back while he determines what should go and what should stay.

The process is not an easy one. At times we will respond with tantrums, like spoiled children. We will want to argue with God. We won't like it when he points out those things we should leave behind. We will wince when we hear him say, "Take no bread, take no bag, and no extra tunic." We will instinctively hug our bank books and cringe when he says, "Take no money."

When I feel those twinges of pain, I often think about my children packing for college. I remember arguing with Matt about his paintball gun. He just didn't get it. But I was the parent, and it was so obvious to me: a dormitory filled with a thousand teenage boys has to be the worst possible place for a paintball gun.

The infinite wisdom of God knows what is important, what is superfluous, what is detrimental to the life of his disciples. He knows what will slow our progress and what will impede our joy. He is committed to doing whatever it takes to pour his omnipotent, extravagant goodness into our lives. The cross and the empty tomb prove this single, most magnificent truth. The disciplines of simplicity and sacrifice enable us to make room for it.

5

~

LIVING IN ANTICIPATION

THE DISCIPLINES OF FASTING AND CHASTITY

*C*hristians don't have to fast anymore, do they?" The question came from a young woman who pursues an active life of faith. "What's the point of it?" she wondered.

Good question. She hadn't known many Christians who fasted, had never been encouraged to fast herself, and frankly, she couldn't see how it could be significant for her spiritual life.

She's not alone.

It is a rare church that encourages its members to fast. My friend Alan is unique in his experience with this discipline. He grew up in a church where both Sunday school teachers and pastors spoke often about fasting. Their example was John Wesley, who fasted twice a week, every week. But in recent decades, among most Christian denominations, the discipline of fasting has lost importance.

In more than half a century of church attendance (my mother used to nurse me while she taught her women's Sunday school class), I've never heard a pastor encourage his congregation to engage in regular, private periods of personal fasting. I've heard an occasional sermon suggesting that a congregation fast at the beginning of a building program—usually so all members can prayerfully consider how much they will commit to a faith-pledge card. One conservative Bible church I attended asked members to fast and pray for a day during their search for a new pastor. But this was a first-time experience for most of the Christians in our fellowship.

It is as though the church has decided that fasting is no longer relevant to an active life of faith. I don't know how we arrived at that. Certainly, Jesus never said or did anything to make us believe that fasting would eventually become irrelevant to his followers during the "church age." In fact, he said exactly the opposite.

Remember the time John the Baptist's disciples approached Jesus? "We fast," they said. "And so do the Pharisees. Why don't your disciples?" Jesus' answer is fascinating. "How can the guests of the bridegroom mourn while he is with them? The time will come when the bridegroom will be taken from them; then they will fast."[1]

"You don't fast while I'm here," Jesus was saying. "You fast when I'm gone."

Jesus is no longer physically present; he resides in heaven at the right hand of the Father. It is time to fast.

Why Fast?

The Bible is full of examples of fasting. The Old Testament shows us Israel fasting and praying innumerable times—often in dangerous circumstances. Other times, individuals fasted as they prayed about specific struggles and temptations in which they needed to be single-minded in their pursuit of God.

David the shepherd-king fasted. Daniel fasted. Esther the queen fasted. Moses and all of Israel fasted. In the Gospels we see Jesus fasting. In Acts we see the leaders of the church, including Paul, fasting.

Each account of fasting derived from a deep sense of need: for safety, for guidance, for comfort, for an outlet for grief and mourning, for spiritual power, for increased strength and courage to meet an unusual challenge. It's not hard to see what Jesus meant when he said the disciples had no need of fasting while he was physically present with them. They were eating, sleeping, working alongside Omnipotence. By *not* fasting, they were figuratively feasting on the Bread of Life, celebrating the joy of the Bridegroom, participating in the prewedding activities, enjoying the promise of the future.

Although the Incarnation was heaven's loss for thirty-three years, it was earth's gain, mankind's salvation. The Potter became clay. God in human form walked and talked with us. He left footprints in the desert sand. His fingers caressed palsied limbs and massaged lepers' skin.

The warmth of his touch lingers, but Jesus no longer walks among us as he did two thousand years ago. The Bridegroom returned to his Father's house to begin a building program of his own. He's adding rooms to his Father's house, rooms that his bride will share with him.

He is not physically present with us, and we have reason now to fast. We miss him! We yearn for his return! We want always to be thinking of him, although we can't see him; remembering that he is coming again, although we don't know when. Fasting reminds us of that truth.

What Does Fasting Look Like?

"When you fast, do it in secret." Jesus' comment in Matthew 6 was prompted by the embarrassing show of false humility put on by the Pharisees when they fasted. Walking through the streets, they twisted their faces into miserable masks so that everyone who looked at them would think how spiritual they were for starving themselves for God. They weren't focused on worship, on undistracted attention to God, but rather on garnering the approval and amazement of all who saw them. (They obviously didn't recognize the Bridegroom among them.) And Jesus was offended.

"Fasting should be done in secret," he told his disciples. "Don't put on a show. If you're fasting, no one should be able to tell." That's what fasting should look like for a believer who has committed herself to a particular time of individual fasting. (Chapter 6 will address this more fully in the discussion of the discipline of secrecy.)

Corporate fasting, those times when a church or community calls its people together to fast, will not be secretive in the same way, but neither should it be a time for believers to draw attention to themselves. It should be a time when, as John Piper wrote, we worship by "preferring God to food in fasting."[2] It should be a time when we express our yearning for the reality of the invisible kingdom of God, when we subjugate our physical appetite in order to more fully experience and identify our spiritual hunger. We fast and allow every hunger pang to remind us that we are not physical only, but spiritual. In the same way bread sustains our physical life, the Bread of Life sustains us spiritually.

The prophet Jeremiah made this important point about fasting: it is never to be a substitute for obedience, or a ritual prac-

ticed out of a rebellious heart. The nation of Israel, boldly
engaged in deliberate sin, prompted God to say, "Although they
fast, I will not listen to their cry."[3] The message is clear: fasting,
the mere act of giving up food, doesn't impress God. "The sacri-
fices of God are a broken spirit; / a broken and contrite heart, / O
God, you will not despise."[4]

What Happens When We Fast?

My sister-in-law, Kathy, and her pastor-husband, Doug, fasted
before making the decision to allow their eighteen-year-old
daughter to move to New York City to attend school and study
acting.

"We fasted for three days and then came together to discuss
what we felt God was saying to us. Both of us had the distinct
impression that God was asking us to trust him, that he would
work out the details. We were to let her go. That decision went
against everything I am as a person and as a mother, but we both
felt it was right."

Kathy also told me about her decision to observe Lent this
year, for the first time. It was a kind of fast, deliberately eliminat-
ing certain foods (favorites) from her diet for the Easter season.

"It was a remarkable experience," she said. "Whenever I
came to the decision of saying no about a food, it was such a great
spiritual exercise to contemplate what Christ had given up for
me by coming to earth. Passion Week was more meaningful to
me than it has ever been.

"It was such a miniscule thing, but one thing I gave up was
coffee, and as I thought about how much I would enjoy drinking
a cup of coffee at lunch on Easter, I reveled in the joy of Christ
looking forward to the resurrection, knowing what it would mean

for all mankind. I felt a new agony on Friday during the crucifixion hours. It all just seemed so much more real to me because of observing Lent, which is its own kind of fasting."

How well I remember my first fast. It was during a time of personal sorrow for me. I was struggling over issues within my family and decided to try fasting. Maybe God would do something extraordinary in response, I thought.

For forty-eight hours I drank water and listened to my stomach rumble. I prayed almost without ceasing and let every hunger pang remind me that I was doing a good thing, that it would be worth it, because God was going to act in a supernatural way on my behalf because I had fasted. At the end of the fast, I sank into a chair, hungry, disappointed, and thought, *Nothing*. Nothing happened. Nothing changed.

I'm not sure exactly what I expected, but God hadn't spoken to me. I felt angry, confused. It took a while for me to understand that something *had* happened inside me during that time of fasting. When I was able to identify it, I was ashamed. While I had thought I was fasting in order to hear God, I was really fasting in order to get God's favor, to persuade him to do *my* will.

It should have been an intimate time of fellowship with the Father and an expression of my yearning for him; it should have been a time of focusing on the reality of his invisible kingdom and the coming wedding celebration. It should have been a time of listening and worshiping. Instead, I turned it into an attempt at manipulation and bullying. (As if as clay, I could bully the King of kings!)

How little I understood about the discipline of fasting. Some months later, with a different heart and a different understanding, I tried fasting again. I was struggling with fear and disappointment. I wondered if God was ever going to restore my joy.

The decision to fast at that time rose from an intense need to *hear* God, not to shout at him. I was at a place in my faith that I can describe only using Brennan Manning's words: "Faith means you want God and want to want nothing more."[5]

I wanted to want nothing more.

Early one morning, in the second day of what I had intended to be a three-day fast, as I went to my knees in prayer I began sobbing. My heart was broken over people I loved, circumstances that could never be made right, loss and sadness that seemed like it would never leave my soul. And then, suddenly, in the middle of the storm of tears, the soft voice of God reached my spirit. It was an unforgettable voice, inaudible, but powerful in my heart.

"Get up. Wash your face. Eat breakfast and get to work."

I lifted my head, looked around, and tried to focus tear-blurred eyes.

I knew I had heard the words. The instructions were clear.

"Get up off your knees." *Okay, I can do that,* I thought. And I splashed water on my face.

Next: eat breakfast. Break the fast I had begun? Hmmm, this was curious, but I went into the kitchen and stuck a muffin in the toaster oven and ate it while standing at the counter. A few minutes later I was at work at my desk.

I was certain God had told me to do those four things. Why, I wasn't sure, but I had no doubt he had spoken to me and told me to stop fasting.

It wasn't until later that day that I understood the significance of what had happened. I remembered what Jesus had said to John's disciples. "Why should the friends of the Bridegroom mourn while he is with them?"

Gently, unmistakably, God told me, "The Bridegroom has come. I am with you. Stop mourning over this situation. Don't let it rob you of joy and deprive you of hope. Eat! This isn't a time to fast, but to feast on the joy of the Lord. The Bridegroom is with you!"

I will never forget the joy that enveloped me in that moment of understanding. Jesus, my Bridegroom, was present, in the form of his Holy Spirit. I was not alone. The load of sadness lifted. It was time to stop grieving and step into the dance.

At that moment, I wanted God. Only God.

I didn't ask for an account of what the future held. I wasn't concerned about what God was going to do to resolve the painful issues that had troubled me. In that space of time, hedged about by the love of God, the only thing that mattered was that God had made himself real.

At the beginning of the fast, I had wanted to want only God. Halfway through it, I was hungry, yet satisfied as I had never been before. Empty, yet full. God had fed me, and nothing else mattered.

I am at times still tempted to grieve over the same family matter that prompted that period of fasting, but then God reminds me that he specifically instructed me *not* to grieve over that anymore. That he is present in that circumstance, and it is time to feast on his sufficiency.

Indeed, there is a time to fast, and a time to feast.

Fortified by Fasting

Jesus fasted before his time of temptation. The story is well known to Christians everywhere.

After forty days of not eating, Jesus had to confront Satan and a battle for the kingdom began. For years I've heard pastors and teachers say, "How like Satan, that wily villain, to approach Jesus during his time of great weakness. Satan probably thought, *Aha! I've got him while he's down—an easy win!*" We are supposed to conclude then that Satan will attack us when we are at our weakest.

I'm sure it's true that Satan does come after us during such times. It's just good war strategy. But I think in the matter of Jesus' temptation, Dallas Willard's proposition in *The Divine Conspiracy* may be more accurate. Consider this: could it be that Jesus was stronger, better able to meet the attacks of Satan *because* he had been fasting? *Because* he was so totally aligned with his Father, so certain of the kingdom of God and his sovereign place in it, and so perfectly in tune with his Father's voice?

Scripture gives strong evidence that fasting creates spiritual strength. Remember the incident in the Gospels when Jesus' disciples tried to cast demons out of a young boy and couldn't? Jesus said that for them, prayer with fasting was necessary in order to duel with Satan in that instance.[6]

It isn't the fact of being hungry that strengthens us, but rather that feasting on God alone strengthens us. As we recognize him as the source of life and let go of all other ideas of strength and sustenance, God energizes us for spiritual battle. He uniquely empowers us for meeting temptation. He uniquely enables us to hear with spiritual ears. He specifically equips us for obedience.

Jesus was hungry, yes, when Satan came to him. It's no coincidence that Satan's first volley was to try to convince Jesus to turn stones into bread. It will always be so when the tempter comes to us. He will always tempt us to turn something less into God. We can resist him only if we recognize our true and deepest hunger is for God.

Fasting teaches us to recognize our true hunger and to identify our greatest source of strength.

How Do We Fast?

How does one initiate a fast, given the lifestyle we live, the lack of privacy we often endure, the social obligations that rule our lives? How does one fast if medical concerns are a factor?

The good news is this: anyone, regardless of health, environment, and chaotic schedules, can fast. And in fasting, he or she can experience the sufficiency of God.

For those who for medical reasons cannot do an absolute fast, we can turn to the example of Daniel, who fasted by committing himself to what I call "simple fare."[7] This has worked well for me on many occasions. I plan a day, or several days, to follow a regimen I call "a day of prayer and simple fare."

I make a plan and commit to eating foods that will nourish me for work and allow me to get through whatever social obligations I can't avoid while still enabling me to fast in secret. I can order off a menu or come home and prepare a meal for my family and myself, and still be in a continual fast by limiting myself to basic foods I have committed to eat. I decide ahead of time what will constitute my meals during this kind of fast. I usually limit it to certain vegetables, fruit, or salads, or soup. Many Christians who struggle with diabetes or hypoglycemia tell me they fast the same way.

My friend Nancy once shared a day of fasting with two very close Christian friends. She had told them about a matter that was troubling her and the couple committed to spend a day fasting and praying for her. Nancy decided to join them.

"I chose a passage from the Twenty-third Psalm and meditated on it all day. I was home from work that day and had the freedom to meditate for hours. I visualized Jesus as my Shepherd, preparing a safe place for me and leading me toward it. But before I could go in, he told me to unload the burdens I'd been carrying. I remember just feeling as though I was emptying my pockets, dumping out stones I'd gathered that were weighing me down. It was a very freeing thing for me. I really did release my burdens to him.

"God didn't specifically address the matter that had prompted me to pray and fast. He didn't say, 'Okay, I'll do what you're asking.' He didn't give me any specific promises about what he would do about my request in the future. But he did give me total assurance that he is my Shepherd and I can trust him. That I belong to him. I know I'm his. And that was enough."

This is the message that comes through to us when we fast prayerfully, seeking God to make himself real to us: Jesus is with us. Sometimes there is a dramatic sense of the presence of God. Sometimes there is only the quiet assurance of his sovereign love that comes after a time of focusing on him, remembering his love and sacrifice for us, recalling his promise to come back for us and take us to his Father's home for a grand wedding feast.

Sometimes a fast ends with only the knowledge that we have spent time focusing on the spiritual realities that too often are lost in our chaotic efforts to tend to the physical.

The point is to follow the example set by Jesus, who is our Master, and the example of godly people through the centuries who found it important to abstain from food, or certain foods, in order to focus more completely on God. And in those occasions, they discovered, as Jesus once told his disciples, that there is "food to eat that you know nothing about."[8]

God himself feeds us with nourishment that strengthens our

souls. He reminds us of his presence and calls us into fellowship with him, invites us to share in his ministry through fasting and prayer. He reveals truth to us that we might not learn in any other setting. Is this not reason enough to push away from the table?

Jesus Is Fasting Now

Imagine this: Jesus, at this very moment, is engaged in a fast. It began on the night of Jesus' betrayal, as he had supper with his closest friends. "I tell you, I will not drink of this fruit of the vine from now until that day when I drink it anew with you in my Father's kingdom."[9]

Today, seated at the right hand of the Father, Jesus prays for us and continues his fast. In the same way our fasting illustrates the physical absence of our Bridegroom and our yearning for him, his fast tells us that he longs for us, that he never forgets for a moment that we belong with him, and that he too yearns for the day when we will share his kingdom, reigning with him as his bride.

On that day, he will pop the cork on the finest vintage and we will drink a toast to redemption, to romance, to holiness, to joy unbounded and unending.

Until then, we fast. He fasts.

We yearn. He yearns.

And we wait, as he waits, for the moment when the Father sends him for us.

The Discipline of Chastity

Chastity reminds us that we are betrothed, that a wedding awaits us. It reminds us that we belong to the Bridegroom, Jesus Christ. It calls us to live in a way that will demonstrate our total commitment to the pledge he has made to us, through his life and his blood.

The discipline of chastity calls us to fidelity—in our physical lives as well as our spiritual.

To the godly woman, the discipline of chastity says, "Don't give yourself to any man who has not done for you what Christ has done—committed his very life to you, giving himself to you as your husband, vowing to live with you in purity and fidelity."

It says, "Discipline your behavior in such a way that it is obvious that you are committed to God, by your manner, your conversation, your entire demeanor. Let there be nothing in your behavior or your words that would suggest that you would violate the purity to which your Bridegroom, Christ, has called you."

The Magnificent Metaphor

I have lots of wonderful single women I count as friends. Many of them are godly, talented women who often wonder why God hasn't allowed them the joy of marriage and the experience of sexual intimacy. No one can answer that question. It is one that God himself will have to address when we step into his palace. But I love how John Eldredge answered a group of single women who approached him during a lecture series he was giving on the topic of eternity. Their question: Will there be sex in heaven?

Like many single women I know, they were struggling with the idea that, after a lifetime of chastity, they would eventually end their earthly lives and enter eternity, never to experience the mysterious bliss of sexual intimacy.

Eldredge answered that sex, essentially, is an expression of worship. It is a magnificent metaphor for the deepest intimacy imaginable.

He reminds us of that beautiful old wedding vow, "With my body I thee worship." Those words will ring through the halls of heaven with new meaning one day.

Eldredge wrote:

> To give yourself over to another, passionately and nakedly, to adore that person body, soul and spirit—we know there is something special, even sacramental about sex. It requires trust and abandonment, guided by a wholehearted devotion. What else can this be but worship? After all, God employs explicitly sexual language to describe faithfulness (and unfaithfulness) to him. For us creatures of the flesh, sexual intimacy is the closest parallel we have to real worship. Even the world knows this. Why else would sexual ecstasy become the number one rival to communion with God? The best impostors succeed because they are nearly indistinguishable from what they are trying to imitate.[10]

As I shared Eldredge's thoughts with my Bible study, which was composed mostly of single women, one of them dropped her head on her arms and cried quietly for several moments. I waited, praying silently. Finally, she lifted her head, sniffed, and swiped at her tears.

"I've been really struggling with my singleness—I never expected to be this age and be unmarried. I always wanted a husband, a family. This thought about worship, and intimacy in heaven—it means so much to me." Overcome with emotion, she dropped her head again and continued to weep.

God calls us, *all* of us, married and unmarried alike, to chastity in anticipation of the wedding that awaits us in heaven. And if Eldredge is right, my chaste single friends should have no worries about having "missed out." Nothing *any* of us has experienced in terms of joyful intimacy in this life will compare to the wholehearted, uninhibited worship that will one day cause us to throw ourselves into the arms of our Beloved with all the exuberance and joy of a new bride.

What Chastity Looks Like

If we are unmarried, we save ourselves for that moment, remaining faithful to the one who calls us his own, his betrothed. If we are married, we recognize that the sexual relationship we enjoy now in this body is a beautiful gift, but it is also a metaphor, really only a shadow of what we will experience one day with our Bridegroom, Jesus Christ.

John Piper wrote, "Caring sexuality in marriage magnifies Christ as the great lover of His Bride, the Church."[11]

Today, in our bodies, we enjoy the gift, living in fidelity and love with the one to whom we are joined in this life. For the married woman, the exercise of chastity looks like this: she is faithful to the husband God has given her, acting out in her marriage the picture of her fidelity to Christ. Because he is faithful, she is faithful. She lives in a committed relationship, careful to work to maintain and protect the sacred intimacy God has blessed her with.

For all believing women, married and unmarried alike, chastity means paying attention to our behavior because in our bodies we represent the purity of Jesus Christ. We are careful to watch our body language, our conversation so that we never give anyone a reason to think we would violate the relationship we share with our Lord, the Lover of our souls.

Great freedom exists in this expression of chastity.

I love the way Dallas Willard put it:

To practice chastity, then, we must first practice love, practice seeking the good of those of the opposite sex we come in contact with at home, work, school, church, or next door. Then we will be free to practice the discipline of chastity as appropriate and gain only positive results from it.[12]

For all of us, the exercise of chastity begins in the mind. It begins with the deliberate, Spirit-powered effort to discipline the thoughts that steer our behavior. It means making choices about what we watch, what we read and study, what we allow into the playground of our minds.

A woman I once knew lost her job because she failed to keep a close guard on her mind. A professing Christian, she began surfing the Internet during her coffee breaks and on her lunch hour at work, venturing into several explicitly sexual websites that encouraged her to "chat." When her boss discovered she was using the company computers to visit pornographic sites, he fired her.

But it wasn't only her career that suffered. In a short time, her family life unraveled as well. Bored, careless, she stopped exercising the discipline of chastity, and the snowballing effects of her failure devastated her marriage.

When Chastity in Marriage Means Abstinence

Chastity in marriage may also express itself in periods of abstinence from sexual relations with a spouse. Paul wrote about this in his letter to the Corinthian believers, telling them three criteria should mark this exercise of the discipline of chastity:[13]

The first criteria is that a couple should abstain by mutual consent. It is not chastity at work if a wife simply decides she isn't interested in sex anymore. That's unilateral deprivation, and Paul said not to do that.

The second is that abstinence should be for a limited period of time only, so that your self-control isn't stretched to the limits, to the place where you make desperate, foolish, ungodly decisions about sexual activity and damage your marriage.

The third criterion is that the time of abstinence is to be devoted to prayer.

Paul made it clear: it isn't chastity to withhold intimacy from a spouse in order to make a point, or to manipulate or punish. The discipline of chastity opposes such behavior—it seeks to train us to see each other as more than sexual; it defies the premise that we are objects. It reminds us that God cherishes us, that we are spiritual; that our moments of deepest intimacy represent a marvelous mystery and should not be entered into carelessly or selfishly.

Through the exercise of chastity we learn to establish the bedroom as a place of peace and joy rather than a war zone. We learn to view each other as whole beings, made in the image of God, valued as unique creations God deemed worthy of his Son's death.

Does this sound just too holy and impossible? Is the idea of exercising chastity in this way so far out of your realm of experience that it's hard to imagine any couple you know actually doing this?

You're right. We don't hear a lot about this exercise of chastity in marriage—it is a private, intimate experience. But imagine this. A man and woman, both deeply committed to God, encounter some difficult issues in their marriage. Maybe it's money. Maybe they face a major decision. Maybe they are struggling with family conflicts. Suppose this couple agreed to abstain from sex for a week and to use that week to pray specifically about the issue that is challenging them. This they would do without the heat of passion as a factor, and with the understanding that at the end of the week they would sit down together and talk about possible solutions.

Okay, you're right again. Such a scenario would require great maturity and commitment to the truth, to each other, and to the relationship. Such a scenario would shine a bright, clear spotlight on the level of intimacy in the relationship, wouldn't it? Is the couple able to communicate only on a sexual level, or are they able to respond to one another with wisdom and respect outside of the bedroom? Are they using sex as a tool for manipulation and control?

The exercise of the discipline of chastity in marriage reveals many things about us. It shows us what we value in ourselves, and in our spouses—the body only, or the heart, the mind, the spirit? It can also mirror our relationship with God—do we appeal to him only when we feel ourselves in deep need, using him like an object to satisfy our whims, our cravings? Or do we desire to know him, to enjoy his presence? Do we cultivate closeness and intimacy with him because he is our beloved, and we are his?

How hard it is to keep this eternal, invisible reality in mind! We are a culture that says sex is a need, not an urge, not merely an appetite. Everywhere we look we see images promoting sexual activity as the ultimate means to fulfillment and satisfaction. Messages telling us we are not complete, not wholly engaged in the human experience if we are not sexually active bombard us daily.

The messages are powerful. The media is unrelenting. But the truth of the Bible is clear: our bodies are the temple of the living God. We are not our own, we are bought with a price.

How do we wend our way through the bevy of billboards that assault us with sexual come-ons? Every magazine, most entertainment venues, and many commercials defy us to live lives of chastity. How do we withstand the barrage on our souls?

The secret appears in a psalm written by King David.

Commit your way to the Lord;
trust in him and he will do this:
He will make your righteousness
shine like the dawn,
the justice of your cause
like the noonday sun.[14]

I was fascinated to discover that the word "way" David used in this verse also means "sexual vigor." It is the same word used in Proverbs 31:3 to warn King Lemuel about the kind of women who could bring down a king. "Guard your passions," the oracle was telling him, "guard your sexual strength."

Now, read David's psalm again and think about committing your sexual vigor to the Lord. Think about trusting him with your passions, with that most intimate aspect of your being. Then see how God will respond to you: he will make your righteousness shine—as sure as the dawn, bright and healing and revealing—you will not be ashamed when the light hits you. And your discernment will be clear and sharp like the rays of the noonday sun.

God is assuring us, through his servant David, that if we commit our sexual vigor to him, if our passions are under his control, he will establish our righteousness and affirm our judgment. He will make us strong and able to make wise decisions.

This is a powerful principle for every believer. Chastity calls us to submit our passions, our sexual vigor, to the control of the Holy Spirit. And then we can expect God to train us in godliness and teach us good judgment.

As I look at single adults and the challenges and powerful temptations that our culture hurls at them, this is my prayer for them: that they will commit to God their "way" and that he will establish them in righteousness and affirm their judgment.

This is the first verse of my prayer, because singles reside close to my heart, and because the typical view of single life our culture serves them is so distorted.

But in the second verse, I pray for myself as well, and for all of us who comprise the bride of Christ, the church. I pray that we will live in constant yearning for the appearing of our Bridegroom, ready to see him without shame or embarrassment. I pray that we will live lives that are an exhibit of the fidelity and purity of Christ. That our lives will reflect the magnificent reality behind the metaphor.

I pray that we will remember that in the exercise of chastity, there are no "time-outs."

"You are always in a temple. Always worship."[15]

Regaining Chastity

"I craved purity," she said. A former lesbian, activist, and militant defender of abortion rights, the woman spoke softly, calmly, as she talked about her life. "God haunted me for two years."

Her words haunted me. I imagined Jesus, the Lover of her soul, pursuing her, persuading her with love words, assuring her of welcome into his heart, into his family. Finally, she threw herself into the arms of Jesus and found the purity her heart had craved. She discovered that within the circle of his love she could live out chastity, committing her heart and body to the Bridegroom who loved her all the way to the cross.

Some call it "regained chastity." Others refer to it as a kind of second-chance virginity. God calls it forgiveness, restoration—the same thing he calls it when I come to him in my sin, confessing my need, asking for forgiveness. As Brennan Manning says, we are all "ragamuffins," reprobates. We are all broken and in need of a Savior. The nature of our sin may vary, but our sin natures are all the same: depraved, helpless, hopeless.

Whatever our state, we can never fully plumb the depth of God's forgiveness in Jesus. It is deeper than any pit of sin that anyone could ever plunge into.

It was deep enough for the Samaritan woman at the well who had had five husbands (and who knows how many lovers) when Jesus bridged the wide chasm of culture and gender, offering her friendship and the living water.[16] It spilled onto the woman caught in adultery—the woman dragged by the Pharisees and tossed into the dirt at Jesus' feet. "Let the one who is without sin cast the first stone," he said. As her accusers skulked away, Jesus asked her, "Does no man condemn you? Neither do I. Go, and sin no more."[17]

God puts no limits on his forgiveness. He offers it to all of us. The humble, the repentant, receive it gladly, with great awe and trembling. Regardless of our past, our present, even our future failings, his grace is sufficient; his love relentless.

Whatever our condition, God loves us mightily, accepts us absolutely. And it is his love that offers rescue, redemption, and the true romance that our souls long for.

It is never too late to dive into the love of God for cleansing and acceptance. It is never too late to enjoy the freedom and joy of chastity.

A Wedding and a Feast

If sexual intimacy here and now is only a shadowy picture of the intimacy we will experience in eternity, imagine what it will be like to be finally with the Lord! Imagine being ravished by his love!

On that day, when the kingdom of God comes fully and completely, Jesus will open the wine and end his fast.

He will lead his bride to the table of feasting, and the celebration of the Marriage Supper of the Lamb will begin.

May fasting remind us of what awaits us.

May chastity be our worship as we wait.

6

CONTENT WITH HIDDENNESS

THE DISCIPLINE OF SECRECY

I'm a football fan—the result of more than thirty years of marriage to a "jock." Regardless of who's playing, I watch the NFL, along with Ken, our kids, and as many of their friends as we can cram into our family room. I knew I had reached die-hard sports-fan status when I began watching Monday night football alone, while Ken was miles away on business in another city.

Of all the games I've cheered and lamented, Super Bowl XXXIV has to be one of my all-time favorites. It gave sports fans one of the most exciting and memorable finishes in NFL history. In the final seconds, the score was 22–16, the St. Louis Rams over the Tennessee Titans. In a valiant effort to tie the game and give the losing Titans another chance at victory, quarterback Steve McNair threw the football to a receiver who ran a slant pattern only to be tackled on the one-yard line as the clock ran out.

Moments later, amid the noise and chaos and confetti, television cameras caught a poignant picture of Titan coach Jeff Fisher with his arms wrapped around his exhausted, heartbroken quarterback. Crushing him in a bear hug, Coach Fisher was tightening his hold and talking quietly, saying things only Steve McNair could hear.

Later, after the Rams had accepted the trophy, after reporters had asked endless questions of coaches and players, and after TV personnel had dissected every strategic play of the game, a commentator nabbed Jeff Fisher for one final question. "What did you say to Steve McNair when you hugged him at the end of the game?"

Jeff Fisher looked into the camera and said, "I'm not going to tell you that. It's between me and Steve."

It was a momentous occasion in TV land—almost as momentous as the Rams' victory.

In this tell-all age, when strangers go on camera to broadcast the secrets of their private lives, when we can overhear the most intimate matters on cell-phone conversations in the grocery store aisle, the deliberate choice to keep a secret when facing a microphone and TV camera is almost as newsworthy as the Rams' victory.

That day, in front of millions, Jeff Fisher exhibited the forgotten, long-neglected discipline of secrecy. What he didn't say resonated with cultural significance far greater than all the sports clichés and accolades shouted in the aftermath of the Super Bowl.

Jesus Valued Secrecy

You've probably never heard a Sunday sermon titled "The Discipline of Secrecy," but Jesus preached on that topic.

In his Sermon on the Mount, Jesus mentioned secrecy more often than any other subject. In Matthew's Gospel, the sermon fills three chapters, covering a variety of topics. Five verses address the topic of murder, three address adultery, and five instruct us to love our enemies. Jesus spent time on other subjects as well, but only secrecy was spoken of in eleven verses as Jesus applied it to his teaching on service, prayer, giving, and fasting. His repeated emphasis on it tells us that he valued secrecy; that he considered secrecy essential to the kingdom life he taught about that day on the side of the mountain.

It is important today as well.

Why?

Because the discipline of secrecy addresses human ego—our craving for applause and adulation. It calls us to relinquish our urgent need to control others' lives. It draws us into deep levels of trust in God alone. It teaches us to recognize and treasure the intimacy we can enjoy with God.

A Time for Secret Prayer

I winced as I heard the words of the prayer: "Lord, your Word is so clear on this matter of tithing. Thank you for making us able to tithe, as you command. And for all those within hearing who haven't learned the blessing of tithing, I pray that you will show them their sin. Amen."

We were a small gathering, and "all those within hearing who hadn't learned the blessing" pointed to just one guy, bless his heart. He had made the mistake of mentioning to the pray-er that he was struggling in this area. Now he was the subject of the prayer, but more than that, he became a victim of spiritual manipulation. The "message" of the prayer was supposed to correct him, change his behavior; instead, it only angered and embarrassed him.

How tempting it is, when we pray in front of others, to shape our prayers into tools for "fixing" other people.

You've heard those prayers before. You may have prayed them on occasion, hoping your teenager is listening, or your spouse, or your friend. You hope he or she will hear the "message" in the prayer and straighten up.

Jesus heard many such prayers. In the synagogue, the Pharisees prayed loudly, drawing attention to themselves, hoping to garner praise and adulation for their vastly superior education and spiritual standing. In their "prayers," they expounded on Scripture that had done little to change their lives, and they thanked God that they were not like their hearers—pathetic, untaught, unclean, and unworthy.

Jesus condemned them bluntly. "Don't be like them," he said. "Pray in secret. Find a private place. Even a closet will do."

Secret prayer purifies our prayers of this kind of manipulation and coercion. We can't plant suggestions in the ears of hearers. We can't preach at them, shame them, or coerce them into becoming the people we want them to be. We have to trust God, who hears in secret, to do the work himself, with no help from us. We learn that God wants to shape our loved ones into his image. We give up trying to shape them into ours.

We give up the desire for control over others.

We let God be in control.

When we go into a closet to pray in secret, we learn that God can work in the lives of people we love without our interference. He can pinpoint the places that need change without our "preaching" prayers. He can work through his Holy Spirit to accomplish what no amount of manipulation under the guise of "spirituality" could ever do.

We learn that God is enough.

Of course, if we pray in secret we will have to give up our desire to be noticed. We will have to forgo the ego satisfaction of having others regard us as "spiritual" as they listen to the fancy theological terms we plant in our sermonesque prayers.

We will have to stop seeking the approval of others. We will have to learn to derive our contentment from God's approval alone. But the lessons God teaches us through secret prayer are far more valuable than any amount of admiration heaped on us because of the eloquence of our words and the timbre of our voice as it echoes in a sanctuary or on a street corner.

As we pray in secret, in faith, trusting God to do his work, we also learn patience. We learn to recognize God's respect for the dignity of human will. As he gently works with others in response to our secret prayers, we see those changes we yearn for. And we have to say again that it was God alone who did it.

I remember as a child hearing a story of the great missionary Hudson Taylor who once found himself broke and bewildered about how God would take care of him. He decided to tell no one about his need, even though there were those he could have turned to for help. Instead, he prayed in secret, asking God to take care of him in whatever way would best glorify God. After praying alone, Hudson went to bed and slept in peace. The next morning he found an envelope under his door containing the exact amount of money he needed.

That experience taught Hudson Taylor that God could be trusted, that God was sufficient. Soon after, Hudson left for China, where he spent most of his life. The founder of the China Inland Mission, he learned early in his ministry that God is enough.

This is a profound lesson for every believer. I have had several prayer occasions when only God could have delivered, but one of the most poignant involved my daughter, Molly. A recent college graduate, she had moved home to live and attend law school. As adult life crowded in on her and schoolwork and relationships grew complicated and overwhelming, I began to pray secretly that Molly would learn of God's joy.

Over a period of weeks, I saw tiny sprigs of joy in her spirit, like the green tips of hyacinths promising blooms in spring. Then one day, during a snatch of conversation, Molly told me about a "what if" game she had played with a gang of singles the night before. One of the questions before the group was this: What if you had to give up all emotions but one—which one would you keep?

Molly told me the answer she had given: "I wouldn't want to live my life without joy."

She swept quickly out of the room to study, so she didn't see my tears. I was overwhelmed. God had heard me when no one else had. Only he could have done the work in her heart that produced joy.

Nothing is more faith-building than knowing that God has worked for us—God, and God alone.

Regardless of what our culture may tell us, this is what our spirits really desire: firsthand knowledge of God, experience with his tenderness, his love, his amazing power. It's not the sound of human clapping we want, not really. Although we may pray with grandiose words and tremulous voices, it is God's voice, his words our hearts crave.

Secret conversations with God teach us this better than any theology class, better than any sermon.

A Time for Public Prayer

What would Sunday services be like without public prayer? And Sunday school classes, when friends pray aloud for one another?

The teaching on prayer in secret doesn't forbid prayer in

community. Jesus prayed aloud in public. Among his disciples, in the upper room, he prayed. On the mountain, he blessed the food as he multiplied it and fed the crowds. The only time he bashed public prayer was when the people "praying" were using it to accomplish their own ends.

Our worship services would be the poorer if we left out corporate prayer. Our fellowship in small groups would be weakened if we never prayed together.

But imagine how much more effective public prayer would be if those who have occasion to lead us were men and women who had spent hours in secret with the Father, where they had learned to seek nothing but God's glory. There they had learned the truth that God is enough for any situation. That he needs nothing, and no one, to add to his sufficiency. That God alone is deserving of our worship. Then, as they led us into the throne room of grace, their example would be one of pure worship, true humility, and absolute trust in God.

In secret, we learn to pray, seeking just God's glory and being satisfied with him and him alone. We learn to trust him with our lives, and the lives of those we love.

Where Intimacy Occurs

Does anything capture the imagination more than the idea of lovers meeting in secret?

Clandestine meetings in secret places are carefully planned, meticulously guarded. Lovers anticipate them and eagerly rush to them with trembling excitement. Could this be part of what God had in mind when he told us to pray in secret? "Plan those moments to be alone with me," he whispers. "Rush toward the place of meeting with all the excitement of a lover running to meet her beloved, hoping no one will follow to intrude upon those special moments."

It is in secret that lovers exchange their most intimate thoughts. It is in secret that they tell their stories, whisper their words of love—not at the dinner table, surrounded by others, or in a building filled with a thousand people once a week. It is in secret that the deepest moments of intimacy occur, not in the presence of others.

Perhaps these were the thoughts of Charles Bridges, a young preacher, when in 1827 he wrote: "Watch the first step of departure [from God]—the neglect of secret prayer."[1]

A lover fails to come to the special secret meeting place at the appointed time. Her beloved watches, waiting, wondering if her heart has begun to harden against him. Does she prefer the company of crowds, rather than moments alone with him? Does she love another? Does she fear being alone with him because he knows her so well, so intimately, and she knows he will sense even the subtlest change in her heart?

Jesus asks us to meet him in secret. He calls us to a lovers' rendezvous where we can listen to the love that pulses in his heart. When we ignore his invitation, although it may seem merely a small act of rejection, a hard place forms in our hearts. We set foot on a path of departure. He who was once my intimate companion becomes little more than a casual acquaintance I greet once a week with a nod and a smile. Mystery dissolves.

To always relegate prayer to a group activity is to miss out on the most precious interaction the human soul can experience: that of communion with our Lord who calls us his beloved. Never to pray in secret is to hold our Lover at arm's length, when what he desires above everything is to enfold us and whisper for our ears only, "I love you, I love you, I love you."

If we want to know God, to experience him and live in the reality of his love, we must remember this truth:

Intimacies are exchanged in secret, not in a crowd.

Good Deeds Done in Secret

One Sunday morning, during an especially meaningful time of worship, I felt as though my spirit were so alive in Christ, so full of his love and fellowship, that I would burst. When the soloist began singing the anthem "All Rise," the message of the words and the majesty of the melody so overwhelmed me that, almost against my will, I just stood up as though yanked to my feet.

My eyes closed, my heart burning, I was only vaguely aware when my husband stood up alongside me. Then, on the other side, a woman stood; then another, and another. The sound of hundreds of people shuffling to their feet whispered throughout the sanctuary. At the end of the song, the entire congregation was standing, all of us in awe of the beauty and grandeur of our God.

When we sat down in unison, I felt as though I had taken part in a grand moment of worship. I said nothing about it to anyone, not even to Ken, yet we both sensed that a very special event had occurred that had led an entire congregation in visible worship of our invisible God.

A week later I was having lunch with a friend from church. She mentioned the recent Sunday service.

"Someone stood up during the choir anthem," she told me. "Then, one by one, everybody in the congregation started standing up. It was the most moving thing that's happened in that church in a long time.

"I heard that in the second service, the leaders at the front of the church stood as soon as the song began, but it wasn't the same. In the first service, it happened spontaneously.

"Someone said that a woman in the back stood up all alone—no one knew who it was—but by the time the song ended the entire congregation was standing. It was an amazing demonstration of worship.

"Were you there?" she asked.

"Oh, yes, I was there," I said. "I was the lady in the back."

Immediately, something broke inside me. Like the shattering of a Waterford trophy, the breaking was irreparable, the prize irreplaceable.

How badly I wanted to take back the words, but the secret was out. Over the next few moments of conversation, I received the praise of a lovely woman who thought it was "really great" that I had had the courage to stand up when everyone else was sitting down—we're not that kind of church. But her praise was like a painful cacophony compared to the beauty of God's voice when I had contented myself with his approval. There is no way to describe what I lost that day.

Jesus told us to do our "righteous acts" in secret. "Don't let anyone know what you have done." How difficult this is for us because we so crave the adulation of our peers.

Whether in church, or at home, in the workplace, or in the marketplace, we confront scores of opportunities to do righteous acts in secret. It may be an act of worship on a Sunday morning, or the act of filling the saltshaker in the kitchen; it may be making a small repair that goes unnoticed at the office, or making a large donation to a crisis pregnancy center. Whenever God presents us with an opportunity to serve, he wants us to do it for him, not for others' praise.

"Be careful not to do your 'acts of righteousness' before men, to be seen by them," Jesus said. "Do not let your left hand know what your right hand is doing."[2]

In Jesus' day, it was common for the Pharisees to ring bells to announce to the community that they had given money to beggars. Sometimes trumpeters walked with them along the streets and blasted their horns when a Pharisee was about to perform a "righteous act."

We can shake our heads and laugh at such an extreme example of self-worship, but how often we are guilty of the same spirit, if not the same degree of egotism.

A friend told me about attending a church where the pastor asked the top ten givers to stand so everyone could thank them with applause. It's difficult to know who was more offensive to God, the pastor who asked them to stand, or the ten who stood.

How often do we tell others about our good deeds, hoping our status will be quickly elevated a notch or two in their eyes?

Richard Foster wrote: "Self-righteous service requires external rewards. It needs to know that people see and appreciate the effort. . . . True service rests contented in hiddenness."[3]

Can't you imagine Jesus' expression as the Pharisees, with their entourage, paraded through the streets, pausing on corners to drop a coin or two into a beggar's cup, accompanied by the music of trumpets? Jesus, the Son of God, watched these men grab for glory, taking for themselves the praise that was due the Father. He watched them pervert acts of righteousness by turning them into acts of self-aggrandizement.

Are we so different? We may not have trumpets blaring to announce our good deeds, but how tempted we are to look around and hope we've been seen, to hope for applause, or at least a raised eyebrow and a nod of approval when we have done a kind act or performed a service.

When Jesus taught us to do our righteous acts in secret, he was offering us "a way of escape" from the strongest temptation that any of us ever face: elevating ourselves above God and claiming for ourselves the glory that is his alone.

This was the original sin. Not Adam's or Eve's, but Lucifer's, when he rebelled against the supremacy of God and tried to enthrone himself above God. Every day, a thousand times a day, we face this same temptation. The discipline of secrecy trains us to resist it.

Jesus said, "Do your good deeds in secret." If your right hand doesn't even know what your left hand is doing, you can't take credit for the act. You can't steal the glory only God deserves. The serpent-tempter is already defanged.

"When you give to the needy, do not announce it with trumpets, as the hypocrites do . . . to be honored by men," Jesus said.[4]

"Be content to serve in secret," Jesus was saying. "Leave the trumpet fanfare for the symphony hall."

In other words, don't blow your own horn.

No Comparisons, No Competition

Such service not only allows the glory to go to God, who enables us to serve and provides the resources for it, but it also deconstructs the platform from which we often compare and compete.

A good deed can't be compared to another's, either favorably or unfavorably, if no one knows who did it. Kind acts done anonymously aren't able to set up an unhealthy spirit of competition among individual believers. The church can be busy about the business of representing the heart of God without getting sidetracked by petty squabbles about who is best, who is greatest, and who should be seated where in the kingdom.

Secrecy in service trains us to keep our eyes on God, not on others who might be watching and scoring our performance. It trains us to be content with obedience rather than applause. It trains us to serve God only, and not the expectations or demands of other people.

Fast in Secret

We don't hear a lot about fasting these days (as we saw in chapter 5), but in Jesus' day it was a common activity, particularly among the religious leaders. When Jesus told them they should do their fasting in secret, it seemed a radical statement.

Dallas Willard wrote: "What Jesus is teaching us to do in this important passage [on secrecy] is to be free of control by the opinions of others."[5]

If we are honest, most of us would agree that the opinions of others matter to us. As Christians, we care about how we are perceived by our brothers and sisters in Christ, sometimes to the point of bondage. Jesus' teaching on secrecy offers us freedom from just that.

"Fast in secret," he said. "This will break open the cage that holds you captive to the opinions of others."

The religious leaders made a spectacle of themselves when they fasted, "disfigur[ing] their faces to show men they are fasting."[6] Why? Because they could not imagine life without the applause of men. Like heroin addicts who cannot fathom a day without a fix, they orchestrated their every gesture, their every act, to accommodate the opinions of others.

They were obligated. Bound. Caged. Locked in the futile pursuit of others' approval.

Jesus offers a better way to live. He offers liberty from a life

dependent upon the ever-shifting standards of human evalua-
tion. He invites us to let the discipline of secrecy train us to let
go of the pursuit of others' approval, to seek only the smile of
God.

"When you fast," Jesus taught, "wear your normal expression;
go about your normal routine. Don't be obvious. The only one
who really matters will see you."

Fasting is a discipline we exercise because we want to learn
to recognize our spiritual hunger; we want to learn to experience
God and celebrate his sufficiency; we want to focus on the truth
that we are not physical beings only, but also spiritual. It is not
intended to be a religious performance presented under the glare
of lights to an audience that thunders its applause.

Fasting is a private event, a romantic dinner for two. The
main course is the Bread of Life and the dessert the sweetness of
God's presence.

The discipline of secrecy ensures that it will be just that.

God Rewards Secrecy

Wherever Jesus spoke of secrecy, he mentioned its rewards.

"Your Father, who sees what is done in secret, will reward
you."[7]

In Matthew 6, he described the treasures of heaven as incor-
ruptible. They cannot be lost, or stolen, or destroyed. Plaques,
trophies built by human hands will eventually corrode or break,
or get lost with the rest of the debris we collect over a lifetime.
Applause has to finally subside. But the treasures God promises
will decorate the halls of heaven for eternity, and his approval
will swell our hearts throughout innumerable aeons.

Fénelon wrote: "But one who is humble, who remains hidden, who desires to be forgotten, and is afraid of being sought out by the world, will already in this life be respected for not wanting to be sought out. And eternal glory will be the reward for his disregard for false and contemptible glory."[8]

Along with the promise of future treasures comes the immediate reward, its value beyond calculating: that of increasing knowledge of God. His approval satisfies—we don't need to put on a religious show.

God's power is sufficient. We don't need to manipulate or coerce the people we love in an effort to "fix" them according to our standards.

God's presence is enough. We don't need to rely on any other source for our needs.

But the greatest reward for the exercise of secrecy is the mere fact of sharing secrets with the King of kings who is our Beloved.

Words almost fail me here. I'm boggled at the thought that God wants to share secrets with *me*. He wants me to do things, experience things, and then disclose them to only him and no one else. He wants me to consider him my best friend, my closest confidant. He wants me to be free from things like the need for approval and applause, and competition and comparison, and the temptation to coerce and manipulate.

Of all the benefits of the discipline of secrecy, all the lessons taught and learned, this one overshadows the rest. We can't miss this truth: God is a Lover whose yearning for us dignifies our existence; that in seeking to be our secret-keeper, he bonds with us, infusing our lives with romance and mystery.

THE GREAT ENCOUNTER

MEETING GOD THROUGH SOLITUDE
AND SILENCE

I was sitting in carpool line one day, visiting with a couple of women who leaned against my car as we waited for our children to come out of school.

"We've got Scouts on Tuesday, ballet on Monday and Thursday, and soccer practice three nights a week, then games on Saturday," one mom said.

The other mom echoed a similar schedule and added children's theater, Indian Princesses, and church choir on Wednesdays. Sunday meant church for one of the families. Another mom was looking for a new church. I wondered how she had the energy to look for anything other than a comfy sofa where she could curl up and take a nap. I was tired just listening.

This litany of activity overwhelmed me. We were new to the area. Was this the way every family in Dallas lived? I wondered. At that moment, I vowed not to let my family become that busy.

I wanted my children to come home after school and play in

the yard. I wanted Matt to be able to take his fishing pole to the lake and throw the line in while I fixed supper. I wanted Molly to be able to ride her bike and play with toys and read books. I wanted my children to enjoy times of solitude and silence, the disciplines of stillness that my parents had cultivated in me.

I wanted to be able to be still and quiet myself.

My intentions were good. I knew that, "to the ancients, a loud, overcrowded and hurried life is a secular life."[1] But it wasn't long before I was wrestling with a noisy, chaotic schedule of activities and obligations of my own.

My children were in elementary school and they wanted to be involved in extracurricular activities. Molly wanted to take gymnastics. Matt wanted to play Little League. As time passed, we added piano and guitar lessons, children's choir on Wednesday nights, and soccer practice after school with games on weekends.

I was boarding Tess at the stable near our home, so I rode every day, and the children came on weekends for lessons as well. Summer brought swim team along with tennis lessons and tournaments. With the arrival of fall, school once again took center stage, with homework, friends, and after-school activities filling every waking hour.

In time, children's clubs evolved into youth activities. Ken and I had our own events, as well as the countless kids' sports and parties and activities we enjoyed as spectators, chaperones, or simply tagalongs. It happened gradually, but we became a family that had no idea of what it meant to be still, and even less comprehension of the concepts of silence and solitude.

During those years I was working for a magazine, writing a feature (sometimes two) every month, teaching a women's Bible study, and finishing work on my third book. Ken was traveling about 50 percent of the time, trying to be home for ball games, piano recitals, the events that were important to the kids. He accepted a position on the deacon board at our church and began teaching an adult Sunday school class as well. Our lives were full, frenetic, and at times totally out of control.

It wasn't the way I was raised. I knew better. I grew up in a home that valued silence and solitude. Although I never heard a sermon about the specific disciplines of stillness, my parents modeled a quiet life. And while I never had a room of my own (I always shared with one or both of my sisters), I knew where to find solitude.

But as an adult, I was finding it increasingly difficult to be still, to exercise silence and solitude. And any memory my children had of the disciplines of stillness was buried somewhere back in earlier years, in simpler times.

I remember, during one particularly chaotic season, seeing a calendar the size of a picture window hanging in a friend's laundry room. Every weekday was smeared with ink, every weekend marred with activity. I felt ill. I went home and studied my own much smaller calendar, but it was as badly scribbled upon as my friend's. Suddenly, I began yearning for a place to escape to. I longed for stillness. I wished with all my heart for Black Rock.

Black Rock is a large, rocky butte near Fort Defiance, Arizona, on the Navajo reservation. It rises up like a huge, many-storied cathedral about a mile from the apartment complex we lived in when I was in high school. I used to hike it alone after school when I needed to escape the sound of my mother's piano students mutilating Chopin, Mozart, and Schumann in the living room of our tiny apartment.

I could make it to the top of Black Rock in about half an hour. I clambered up its rough, craggy face, finding footholds and handholds, scraping knuckles, until I reached a ridge that wound around to the back, away from the view of sparse buildings and a narrow highway. There I would perch near the top on a rugged outcropping and stare out at the vivid beauty of the land. Sometimes I sat and sang at the top of my lungs. Sometimes I fantasized about what my life would be like someday. Sometimes I prayed. Sometimes I just sat and strained to hear the sounds of sheep bleating in the distance. Sometimes all I heard was quiet.

After an hour or so, I would stand up, brush the dust off the seat of my jeans, climb down Black Rock, jog home, help with supper and dishes, do homework, and sometimes go back to the school for play practice, debate team, or some other activity. But the inner solace I found on Black Rock went with me, giving me a sense of quiet, of equilibrium.

Dallas had no Black Rock for climbing. I would have to find another place of stillness.

Where better than the Rock of Ages?

The Disciplines of Stillness

The psalmists wrote: "Be still, and know that I am God."[2]

"Be still before the Lord."[3]

What does that kind of stillness look like? Visualize your arms going limp, your hands dropping what they've been holding, and you've got an idea of what the psalmists were trying to convey. Then consider this: the writers of Scripture frequently used the word for "knowing" to refer to the intimacy lovers shared.

Now, hear God whisper, "Drop what's in your hands for a moment and come into my arms."

That's what stillness looks like.

There, wrapped in unconditional love, we snuggle close for warmth and comfort. Alone together, we have eyes only for each other. We deal with the issues in our relationship that need attention. In that private place, with just our Beloved, we rest quietly, not worrying about the things we dropped when we ran to him. In silence, we listen to his love words.

In time, we will have to move back into the company of others. We will pick up those tasks we abandoned in order to open our arms to God. But like a blushing bride who has just emerged from a lover's embrace, we will be flush with the excitement and exhilaration of love's sweetness. Our exuberance for life will be overflowing, and our hearts will burn with the desire to tell others of the wonderful love that graces our lives.

Making Time for Solitude

A newspaper columnist recently wrote about how she sometimes told "white lies" to her children when they were young. "Children aren't allowed in the store in the evenings," she used to say as she hurried out of the house to the grocery store. She figured it was easier to lie than to deal with a child's tears if she told him, "I just really want to be alone!"

It's not only young mothers who struggle to find time alone. We live in an increasingly busy and boisterous culture. For all of us, work is demanding, grueling. We often drag ourselves home after long days, having just enough energy to do a few domestic chores before falling into bed. The cycle of people and activity begins again with each new day.

When (if) the crowds thin out, we want the release and relaxation of a novel, or the Sunday paper, or a movie. Keeping company is the last thing on our minds. Yet solitude, as a spiritual discipline, calls us to keep company with God.

It beckons us to carve out time in our hectic schedules to be

alone with God in a quiet place. It invites us to soak in his presence and be revived and renewed.

The Great Encounter

Throughout the Gospels we see accounts of Jesus withdrawing
from the crowds to be alone with his Father. Luke wrote that he
often withdrew to lonely places to pray.[4]

What better reason to make time to be alone with God the
Father than this: Jesus, God's Son, our example, did it often?

Dallas Willard wrote:

> If we have faith in Christ, we must believe that he knew how to
> live. We can, through faith and grace, become like Christ by
> practicing the types of activities he engaged in, by arranging our
> whole lives around the activities he himself practiced in order to
> remain constantly at home in the fellowship of his Father.[5]

Fellowship with the Father was the consuming passion of the
Son.

How easy it is for us to think of the spectacular events of
Jesus' life as the most defining for him, the events that most dra-
matically articulated for him that he was, in fact, the Son of God.
Yet of all the experiences, I am convinced that his certainty of
his identity as Messiah, as Emmanuel—*God with us!*—emerged
from his time alone in fellowship with his heavenly Father.

We cannot conceive of what it must have been like for Jesus,
as a young man growing up in the house of Joseph in Nazareth, to
live with the growing awareness of his sonship, of his unique and
glorious relationship to Yahweh. What must it have been like to
discover that as the Son of God, he held the power of omnipo-

tence in his hands—hands that once gripped his mother's, that tossed stones and carved sticks in Joseph's wood shop?

What must it have been like for him to stand at the tomb in Bethany and cry out, "Lazarus!" and see his friend come out, grave clothes unraveling behind him?

What must Jesus have felt that day when, amid the crowd, a touch on the hem of his robe sent a force ricocheting throughout his body and spirit, and healing occurred without his volitional act?

To sit on a rock and look out at thousands of people waiting on his every word? To wander through village streets, sought after by a Roman soldier who believed he was a healer, a man with authority with God?

The actions of Christ among the crowds easily amaze us, but it is his solitary moments with the Father that should astound us.

"I have never done anything that my Father didn't tell me to do," he told the Jewish leaders who were disturbed by his miracles. "I tell you the truth, the Son can do nothing by himself; he can do only what he sees his Father doing, because whatever the Father does the Son also does. For the Father loves the Son and shows him all he does."[6]

Everything Jesus did among the crowds the Father first conceived and revealed to the Son during times of solitude. Jesus' life demonstrated the truth of the statement that solitude is "the place of the great encounter." It is the place "from which all other encounters derive their meaning."[7]

Arranging Our Whole Lives

Arranging our whole lives around the activities Jesus practiced means making time to be still before God. For most of us, this will require deliberate planning and effort.

My sister, Susan, is a professional musician and a piano teacher. Her students begin arriving in the early afternoon and it is suppertime before the last one leaves. In addition, she accompanies many soloists, plays for church and civic events, and spends many hours practicing and performing. She also teaches a Bible study and has a full life of activities that whirl around her husband, a motorcycle, and children and grandchildren. Early morning is the time she has set aside as her special time to be alone with God.

"I guard that time ferociously," she told me. "I let the answering machine pick up my calls, and I take my coffee cup upstairs to a quiet place and sit alone with God."

"I'm a night person," another woman shared with me. "I like the quiet late at night, when everyone else has gone to bed. It is as if I have the house all to myself. That's when God and I have the best time together. I know we won't be interrupted."

Morning or evening, God is always ready to meet with us and draw us into quiet fellowship with him. I know that now, but I can remember a time when I felt like a spiritual failure if my time alone with God didn't take place in the early morning.

As a young mother, with a toddler, an infant who was often ill, and a husband who traveled, my morning hours (even the wee ones before dawn) were filled with crying, vomiting, coughing, wheezing, and frequent trips to the doctor. If, on the rare morning, the house was quiet, I fell asleep as soon as my seat met a chair cushion. Of course, when I wakened, Bible on my lap, I felt not refreshed, but guilty.

I knew some Scriptures referred to seeking God in the morning. "O my God, thou art my God; early will I seek thee"[8] is only one of many. And I constantly confronted this inescapable truth: "Beginning with Jesus, there is an undeniable Christian tradition of meeting God first thing in the morning."[9] But for years the only time I had was around noon, when the chaos subsided. Often I read standing up, prayed leaning against the fridge.

But several years ago, when my children were older (and healthier), I began getting up early to meet with God. I set the alarm clock and scheduled an hour alone with God before the children awoke. The first days were an experiment. Would God really meet with me? Would I be able to get through the day after starting so early? Would it be worth the effort?

That first morning, God "met" me in a unique way. The quiet of the early hour, the sense of his presence, the communion we shared—it was so sweet and so precious that I couldn't imagine missing it. After that first morning, I couldn't wait for the next, and the next.

A habit grew out of that first, feeble beginning.

I have never regretted the early morning time I've given to God, when I sit alone with him and shut out all other activities and people. But I also refuse to allow myself to feel guilty, or unwanted, if circumstances force me to schedule that time alone with him at another time in the day.

The God I've come to know through study, prayer, solitude, and the other disciplines, is not one who would refuse to gather me into his arms because I didn't get there until after sunup. Having experienced his love and tenderness, I try not to let anything keep me from our morning rendezvous. But if events prevent that from happening, I know he'll welcome me whenever I get there.

If, however, *sin* keeps us away, if we have preferred the company of others to the company of the King of kings, the best thing we can do is to confess it quickly and move into the arms of God. Our intimacy with him hinges on our humble obedience.

Over time, through the work of grace, I've grown more confident of my place in the presence of God. I've found comfort in the words of those wiser than I: "Do not always strictly confine yourself to certain rules, or particular forms of devotion, but act with general confidence in God, with love and humility."[10] "Heart-shattered lives ready for love / don't for a moment escape God's notice."[11]

Henri Nouwen wrote:

In solitude, we meet God. In solitude we leave behind our many activities, concerns, plans and projects, opinions and convictions, and enter into the presence of our loving God, naked, vulnerable, open and receptive. And there we see that he alone is God, that he alone is care, that he alone is forgiveness.[12]

Choosing Silence in a Noisy World

"One hour of honest, serious thinking is more precious than weeks spent in empty talks," wrote Leo Tolstoy.[13]

John Climacus wrote, "Intelligent silence is the mother of prayer."[14]

Mother Teresa said, "God is the friend of silence."[15]

Isaiah the prophet wrote, "In quietness and trust is your strength."[16]

Whenever I look back through my journal and my stack of index cards, I find Isaiah's verse written over and over again. Obviously, choosing to exercise silence, whether before God or among people, is a challenge for me.

It wasn't difficult to exercise the discipline of silence last winter while I sat one afternoon in a snug ski lodge, gazing out the window. There, with God's majestic creation in view, snow-covered peaks spiking into vivid blue sky, my heart stirred with joy and worship. It wasn't a difficult decision to turn off the television and just soak in quiet beauty and let my heart worship the Creator.

A few months later, I stood on a deserted beach in Maui in the early morning and listened to nature's music. All else was silent, except the pounding beat of the rolling ocean and the seagulls' obbligato. I wasn't tempted to take a Walkman or a cell phone with me when I strolled the beach. The quiet of the morning was enough. I had no desire for conversation. No need for noise.

It's true: some situations lend themselves to the exercise of silence; many don't. Exercising the discipline of silence is often a deliberate decision we must make.

Silence in Worship

David wrote, "Find rest, O my soul, in God alone."[17]

Or, more accurately, "Be silent, O my soul."

How do you get your soul to be silent? The mind never stops, does it? If it did, we'd be dead, so I'm not complaining. But how can we make it hush so we can hear God's voice?

One recent morning, I couldn't get my thoughts to stop stirring. Ideas and worries whirled. "Lord," I prayed, "I can't get quiet. I'm alone with you, but the noise in my head is louder than the crowd at a hockey game. Help!"

In the next instant, I felt prompted to begin praying the phrase, "Jesus is Lord." Over and over again, I said the words, identifying the greatest truth ever revealed to humankind. Jesus the Carpenter from Nazareth, born of a virgin, is the Lord of lords, the King of kings. Over the next few moments, all other thoughts and images faded. The powerful truth of the sovereign lordship of Jesus Christ, the Son of God, permeated my mind. Nothing else invaded that space. Quietness settled on me.

Throughout the remainder of the day I was fascinated (awed to the point of tears) to read and hear references to Jesus as Lord everywhere. In my study, in conversations with friends, in my own spirit as I encountered challenges, temptations, and irritable, impatient clerks and scary drivers, the certainty of Jesus' lordship declawed every attacker. His presence was real to me.

When we deliberately choose to be silent before God, he quiets our thoughts and gives us his. He reminds us of his love, of his sovereign care, of his tender mercies, of all that awaits us in eternity. He gives us encouragement and wisdom, and whispers the ancient stories that for centuries have convinced generations of his power and majesty. He reassures us that no matter what we encounter in our lives, he will be sufficient, that his loving, omnipotent presence will be enough. But silence is a prerequisite for hearing him.

Silence in the Presence of Suffering

My friends Margaret and John Paine are dealing courageously with John's recent diagnosis of Lou Gehrig's disease, ALS, for which there is no cure.

"There are days when I cry a lot," Margaret shared with me. "I think sometimes you have to just come to God and pound on his chest, and know it's okay, that he loves you and won't push you away."

The Psalms are full of chest-pounding: "Day and night I cry out before you"; "My soul is full of trouble"; "I call to you, O

Lord, every day"; "Why, O Lord, do you reject me / and hide your face from me?"[18]

But at some point, usually after our pounding and crying has wrenched the last bit of strength from us, we must fall against the Lord and be still. We must listen quietly to his heartbeat.

"That's not easy for me," Margaret said. "I can pray all day long, but to sit still and listen is really hard. My mind seems out of control. When I'm struggling like that with stillness, I say Scripture—'Be still and know that I am God,' and 'Let not your heart be troubled.'"

It was in the context of trials and temptations that James the Apostle wrote, "Be quick to listen, slow to speak, and slow to become angry."[19] This verse struck me with force a few years ago when a crisis hit my family. I was angry at God and told him so. Day after day I asked for answers, begged for God to explain himself to me, and argued with him about why he wasn't handling things the way I asked. It wasn't by chance that I was reading in James's Epistle.

James's words rang out, and the Holy Spirit confronted me. Kindly, courteously, the Spirit of God whispered to my soul, "Jan, this isn't a time to argue and whine. It's a time to listen. If ever you needed to hear me, it's now. Be quiet. Let *me* talk."

So began a quiet journey. As I entered the "great encounter" each day, I made up my mind to be quiet before God, to read his Word with a listening heart. I began to experience what the prophet meant about deriving strength from quietness and trust.

It's hard to explain it, but unfathomable strength sinks into our souls when in faith we sit quietly before God. Incomprehensible courage pours through our veins. We gain confidence and hope during an experience that can be described only as *mystical*—"that wonderful word we apply to things that have ultimate meaning but elude our understanding."[20]

Silence in the Presence of Others

Proverbs is full of instructions to exercise silence in the presence of others. I know. My father used to hoist me onto his lap and read them *all* to me. It didn't occur to me until many years later that I must have been a very talkative child.

But I wasn't the only one God had in mind when he instructed Solomon, through the influence of the Holy Spirit, to write (gender changes mine): "When words are many, sin is not absent, / but she who holds her tongue is wise."[21] "She who guards her mouth and her tongue / keeps herself from calamity."[22]

I'm living proof of the truth of those words. I've experienced the calamity of saying the wrong thing at the wrong time. I've been foolish and spoken when silence would have been the very best choice. But there have been some moments when I've exercised the discipline of silence—the most memorable ones during the three years our adult daughter lived at home with us while attending law school. One particular occasion stands out boldly in my memory.

Molly and I were talking as mothers and daughters sometimes do, and Molly told me about a situation she was facing. She wasn't asking for advice but expressing concern over what she should do. I looked at her with amazement. The answer was so obvious to me.

I started to blurt out my advice, but suddenly I knew that silence was called for. I wanted to say something so badly I thought my head would explode. Unspoken words burned my tongue.

I'm her mom, I thought. *I'm supposed to advise her.*

But God's Spirit kept whispering, "Shhh, Jan. Don't say a word."

The choice was mine. I could trust God to handle the situation, or I could insist on taking control myself. The issue involved wasn't life-threatening, but I had very strong opinions about it, and it was hard to imagine Molly didn't want or need them even though she was an adult. The struggle to be quiet was almost painful. I felt like I was wrestling with the muscles of my face, almost contorting them with the effort to keep my mouth closed.

"She may be twenty-four," I argued with God, "but she's still my child, and I really ought to give her the benefit of my age and wisdom."

It wasn't easy, but I finally gave up the fight. I agreed, reluctantly, to let God speak to my adult daughter. In that instance I chose silence, with God's help. And God spoke to my daughter, through his Word and his Spirit, and through godly friends.

When I think about it now, I feel overwhelmed. What could be better than to know that my child has heard the voice of God? That Omnipotence interacted with her and made his thoughts known to her? Would I rather it was my voice she heard? Would I rather be the one whose words rang in her ears?

For me, it is a trust issue. Can I be silent and trust God to work in the lives of those I love? A husband, friend, relative?

The discipline of silence, in this context, asks me: Do I have to have control and credit, or can I be silent and trust God to take control and handle this matter with his sovereign grace and power?

It asks: Do I have to be the one who always has the last word, or am I content to let God have it?

What a faith-builder it is for me to exercise silence, in the power of the Holy Spirit, and to see God at work in others' lives, proving his sufficiency and manifesting his sovereignty.

Often silence is a gift we give to others to allow them to encounter God for themselves. It is the way we relinquish control to God, allowing him to be the one who gets the last word.

When my children were very small I used to pray this prayer with them at bedtime: "Lord, let them learn to listen to your voice in their hearts."

God answered that prayer. But he first had to begin teaching me the discipline of silence.

Making Changes

Learning to listen to God, learning to keep our mouths shut, getting up early in order to spend time alone with God—these may be just a few of many adjustments we have to make if we are going to exercise the disciplines of stillness. For some of us, a lifestyle overhaul may be required if we are going to experience the delight of communion with God.

That's what happened to me. Although I had established a habit of meeting God in the early morning, our move to Dallas suddenly jarred me out of that important routine. I know now that it wasn't Texas's fault. Everyone, whether in Dallas or Dalhart, Phoenix or Fresno, can get caught up in too much activity. Every one of us, regardless of where we live, can find herself on overload with no time for quietness and solitude.

For me, the decision to pare down my life was easy. I was exhausted and depleted spiritually. I remembered the sweetness of time alone with God. I yearned for it. So, prayerfully, I considered how I could simplify my life to make plenty of room for the "great encounter." God made it very clear that it was not a time in my life to own a horse. He showed my husband it was not the time for him to serve on a deacon board. With the amount of travel demanded by his job, he didn't need to spend his few evenings in town sitting in a room with a dozen men while his wife and family were at home without him.

Other changes surprised me. God showed me he had someone else to teach the women's Bible study I'd been leading for years. He sent me other directions, giving me Christian writers to mentor and encourage. By the time our children hit the teen years, Ken and I had learned to discipline ourselves so that family activities no longer frenzied our schedules. There were (and still are) seasons of busy-ness, but God continues to teach me to keep my time alone with him a priority. Daily he reminds me that my time with him, that "great encounter," is the most important part of my day.

For me, stillness is not a luxury; it's an essential ingredient to the life of faith. Without it, I stagger and limp along a path that should be filled with dancing.

The Fruits of Stillness

The disciplines of stillness, when exercised in faith and in the power of the Holy Spirit, always yield fruit.

John Bunyan's stillness was enforced. While imprisoned in England for his faith, he wrote *Grace Abounding* and began work on *The Pilgrim's Progress*. Twelve years of stillness yielded some of the richest literature Christendom will ever see.

Madame Guyon was imprisoned in the Bastille for most of her adult life. Her crime: writing in passionate terms about her love for her Lord. Her work, *Experiencing the Depths of Jesus Christ*, stands as one of the most enduring treatises ever written on intimacy with God through the Son, Christ Jesus. It scandalized the staid, stoical religious leaders of late-seventeenth-century France who had never encountered God for themselves.

The prison letters Samuel Rutherford wrote three hundred years ago continue to encourage Christians today. Arrested for his stance against the king of England's heresy, Rutherford languished in a prison in Aberdeen for years, yet never gave up his confidence in God. Writing to his parishioners, he said, "I see grace groweth best in winter."[23]

After a debilitating fall that left her bedridden, Amy Carmichael began writing daily notes to encourage the workers at Dohnavur House in India where for decades she had ministered to orphans. Today I draw strength for my own life from those notes, bound and published in a volume called *Edges of His Ways*.

My friend, the Honorable Sam Johnson (U.S. Congress), spent seven years as a POW in North Vietnam, much of that time in solitary confinement. "I turned my attention toward God," Sam said. "I knew with certainty that He was present in that dark, cramped closet of a cell. He listened when I prayed and He answered me. I was comforted and encouraged. I began to know my Creator in a way I had never known Him before."[24]

None of us would choose such austere circumstances, such enforced stillness. Yet all of us need the disciplines of stillness in our lives, for "when we are noisy and when we are hurried, we are incapable of intimacy—deep, complex, personal relationships."[25]

It is in the solitary moments, hemmed with silence, that we discover the heart of God. Our trust in his goodness grows as we stop our own hustle and bustle to sit quietly and watch his sovereignty at work on our behalf.

When we make time to be alone with God, we discover that his presence fills us with contentment like no other's can.

We quiet our hearts and hear God's voice.

We close our mouths and hear God speak for us.

We discover, again and again, that God is sufficient. That he will take up our cause and work all things together for our good.

But often, the first step is to convince us to be still.

Brennan Manning wrote about practicing the disciplines of solitude and silence while attending a spiritual retreat. After thirteen hours, the truth that rang in his heart was this: "Live in the wisdom of accepted tenderness."[26]

It is a great encounter indeed that yields such knowledge. If the disciplines of stillness offered us nothing else, that would be enough.

8

~

SANCTUARY IN THE HEART OF GOD

THE DISCIPLINES OF PRAYER AND MEDITATION

Biopsy is an awful word.

Even if the outcome is good, just to agree to schedule the procedure you have to face terrifying possibilities. It is enough to wrest peace away from even the most trusting saint.

And I am among the least. I fret easily. You can imagine my state of mind when a recent mammogram showed an irregularity and the radiologist requested a biopsy. After all, my aunt has had breast cancer, my father prostate cancer, and my sister T-cell lymphoma. I figured the chances of anything in my body being benign were poor.

Anxiety overwhelmed me.

Pray, pray! I commanded myself the morning of my biopsy, but my thoughts were too unsteady.

It shouldn't be this hard, I told myself. I learned to pray before I learned my ABCs.

Then, in the next instant an idea surfaced, and in another minute, I was on my knees beside my favorite chair, reciting the ABCs and assigning an attribute of God to each letter in the alphabet.

For the next hour I meditated on everything from God's awesome power to his zeal for the holiness of those he saved by the blood of his Son. When I finished with Z, I started at A again, this time praying for every person who came to mind with each letter of the alphabet. Nearly two hours later I got up, stretched, and recognized that my fears were gone. My mind had found comfort in the presence of God, and I had been able to talk to him freely and listen to his assurances of tenderness and love.

My spirit quiet, my fears calmed, I drove to the hospital. Stillness filled me while the radiologist performed the biopsy. In those hours edged with danger, I discovered the truth that "what happens in meditation is that we create the emotional and spiritual space which allows Christ to construct an inner sanctuary in the heart."[1]

Meditation made space amid the clutter of fear and anxiety. Prayer filled that space with the peace of God.

They work together, prayer and meditation.

Meditation: Considering the Immeasurable Value of God

Charles Swindoll called meditation a "lost art." Understandable. It is a discipline that requires a quiet heart, a heart attentive to God—not always an easy thing to accomplish, as we saw in the study of the disciplines of stillness.

Meditation, as a deliberate mental exercise, concentrates our thoughts on the things of God. We consider the immeasurable value of God, letting our minds become occupied with calculating his goodness. It is a kind of rehearsing of truth as we remind ourselves of what we know of God. The psalmist said it best, I think: "Let me understand the teaching of your precepts; / then I will meditate on your wonders."[2]

We think about a particular truth about God, or his kingdom, that we've learned through study and the other disciplines. And then we rehearse it in our minds, the way a musician does, playing it over and over again until the beauty of its meaning sinks deep into our souls and turns our affections toward God.

We consider the truth, and we mull it over, sipping it, tasting it, relishing the richness of it, drawing nourishment from it.

In Times of Distress

My friend's nasty divorce seemed to be getting nastier. She dreaded the court appearance that would determine custody of her teenage daughter. Her ex-husband had plotted for months to keep the child from her mother, and now finally the matter was to be resolved, but not without misery and cruel, untrue accusations. I wanted to be in the courtroom with my friend that day, but the best I could do was encourage her to pray and meditate on the power and goodness of God.

This is what the psalmist did when "princes also did sit and speak against me; but thy servant did meditate in thy statutes." [3]

This is what my friend did.

"God was with me," she told me after the hearing. "It was horrible, but I sensed his presence. I wasn't afraid. I couldn't have gotten through it without him."

We all face moments when we feel powerless and victimized. In those instances, the truth of God's love, grace, and power is our only hope, our only comfort. Meditating on that truth is our first step toward peace as we become convinced of God's presence and assured of his promise to act on our behalf.

To Touch Transcendence

Imagine spending your days in desert lands, wandering from one water hole to the next, sleeping outside on the ground, and playing nursemaid to a flock of foolish, fragile sheep who don't have enough sense to put their mouths down to drink if the pool happens to be even a little bit choppy.

Sound like a retreat, compared to your daily grind? Think again. The ground is hard, the weather unkind. Sheep stink. They wander away. They fall over and can't get up. Prospects of change, of a promotion, aren't likely.

Day after day, the same routine plays out, always accompanied by the sound of bleating and the stench of dung. This was David's lot. Even after he was anointed king, he lived in the wilderness for years, sleeping in caves, fighting for his life, tramping about with vagabonds and losers. Routine, rebellion, disappointment, the death of expectations—all these things, and more, conspired to dull his soul.

Centuries later, most of us aren't that different. We struggle to achieve, and fail often. We deal with situations that stink and with people who cheer our losses. We live wearying lives, swimming in swill, until something higher than us, something above ourselves, something *noble,* calls us up from the pond, and we reach for it with greedy hands.

Long before he ascended the throne of Israel, David held nobility in grubby, calloused fists. He was awed by God's majesty. He "considered the heavens."[4] He studied them and was stunned by their beauty. He contemplated creation, the magnitude of God's power. And he thought often about the Lord: "I have set the Lord always before me."[5]

Speaking of God's ways, David said, "They are more precious than gold, they are sweeter than honey."[6]

By concentrating on God, focusing his thoughts on the power and majesty of God, David's life, though often messy and strife-filled, was infused with transcendence.

"O Lord, how majestic is your name!"[7]

"Whatever is true, whatever is noble, whatever is right, whatever is pure, whatever is lovely, whatever is admirable—if anything is excellent or praiseworthy—think about such things," the apostle Paul wrote to the Philippian church.[8] Whether he learned it aboard a sinking ship or while chained to a prison guard, he knew meditation was essential to the life of faith. He mulled over the sweetness of God and concentrated on his goodness and mercy, infusing nobility into the most ignoble circumstances and defining contentment for us: "For me to live is Christ and to die is gain."[9]

A Defense Against Mischief

Brother Lawrence wrote, "Our useless thoughts spoil everything. They are where mischief begins."[10] Meditation is where our rescue is accomplished.

It wasn't until I began diligently meditating that I discovered how to have victory over "the sin that so easily entangles" me.[11] For years have I struggled with imaginings that distress me, fantasies that trouble me, and thoughts that trigger depression, irritation, and feelings of futility. Although I have prayed for God's strength and begged him to remove the temptation, at night I often lay my head on my pillow and the thoughts begin to swirl. Thoughts of people, of events, wide-awake dreams of how I wish my life could be, of how I wish others would behave—my mind becomes a factory for discontent, robbing me of the joy of my own reality.

The daylight hours aren't so troubling—I'm busy, I'm working, I'm interacting with people. But at night, when it is dark and silent, and I'm totally alone with this self and its nature, I find it so horribly easy to be unhappy with the person I am and the life I live. Only meditation has been my defense against this insidious sin.

When I am preoccupied with the truth of God and his sovereign plans for me, all thoughts of discontent fly away—almost the instant I choose to meditate on God. My mind becomes filled with awareness of God's tender love for me, and I am quickly at peace, quickly settled, and almost instantly relieved of any desire to think of anything but God.

It amazes me that something so simple as meditation should be the sword that slays my enemy. It is a miraculous thing. It is God at work in me. It is his Spirit who rescues me when I commit my mind to him and allow his thoughts to replace my own errant ones.

I would feel embarrassed about revealing such a stupid sin if it weren't for the fact that every sin is stupid. Rebelling against the holy, all-powerful God!—if that's not stupid, what is? But I am only one of millions of stupid creatures, easily caught up in what we consider to be small acts of rebellion. And each of these begins in our thought life. God promised us a way of escape, so that we would be able to bear the temptation[12]—for me that escape has been meditation.

Charles Bridges wrote:

Learn in the hour of trial where to go, and what to do. Go to the word of God for direction and support. *Meditate in His precepts.* There is often a hurry of mind in times of difficulty, which unhinges the soul from the simple exercise of faith. But habit brings practice, and steadiness, and simplicity, enabling us most sweetly to fix our hearts upon the word of God, and to apply its directions and encouragements to the present [crisis].[13]

Or, in Brother Lawrence's words: Make thinking on God a holy habit.[14]

Nourished by God

"If you wish to keep growing you must nourish in your heart the lively longing for God."[15] Meditation is a vital means of nourishing our hearts.

"No shortcut exists," wrote A. W. Tozer. "God has not bowed to our nervous haste nor embraced the methods of our machine age. It is well that we accept the hard truth now: The [woman] who would know God must give time to Him. . . . [She] must give [herself] to meditation and prayer hours on end."[16]

Hours on end? It sounds daunting, doesn't it? But it can be done. My friend Donna told about making the trip to a Texas town a few hours away from Dallas and meditating the entire drive. "I never turned on the radio," she said. "I just thought about God, prayed, meditated, and the hours flew by."

Short trips about town offer us meditation time. I often leave the radio off when I'm out running errands. It's a quiet time I can use to meditate and pray. If my thoughts are scattered, I use my "alphabet system" to capture my flighty imagination and focus it on the reality of God.

A student I know meditates on God during a yoga/stretching/relaxation class. Conscious of her muscles and tendons reaching, pulling, she seeks biblical truths from the parable of her body. She walks out relaxed, in tune with Jesus Christ, focused on his power and his strength, assured that he will be sufficient for her whatever her circumstances.

Friends tell of meditating on the goodness of God as they walk through crowded malls. I've meditated on his compassion and his sovereign power while folding laundry, walking on a treadmill, maneuvering a cart through grocery store aisles, and sitting in a doctor's waiting room.

Richard Baxter, a Puritan preacher from the seventeenth century, wrote, "As digestion turns food into chyle and blood for vigorous health, so meditation turns the truths received and remembered into warm affection, firm resolution, and holy living. . . . Let it be frequent . . . to prevent a shyness between God and your soul."[17]

The Godly women whose example I treasure are not "shy" before God. They are intimate with him. They make a priority time to mull over the truth of God, to consider his loving-kindness, and to bask in the knowledge of his power that will be at work in their lives throughout the day. Thoughts of God are never far from their minds, regardless of the tasks that occupy their hands. They meditate "in his law day and night." Psalm 1 might have been written to them:

> You thrill to God's Word,
> you chew on Scripture day and night.
> You're a tree replanted in Eden,
>   bearing fresh fruit every month,
> Never dropping a leaf,
> always in blossom.[18]

I want to be described that way—as one who thrills to God's Word, always in blossom. If Scripture is accurate and the lives of saints credible, this can be true of me through the discipline of meditation, through the power of God, who "always fills with blessings a heart that is nourished neither by the world nor by fantasy, but by Him alone."[19]

Prayer: Engaging Omnipotence

Meditation makes me aware of the reality of God. Prayer engages his omnipotence.

Awesome thought, isn't it? Aloud, or in the silence of our souls, we call out to God and in that moment all of his sovereign, magnificent power, all of his extravagant goodness, is brought to bear on our need.

As I write this, I am overwhelmed by the immensity of the mystery of prayer and the sacred privilege of it. Prayer cannot be summed up in a few pages in a book. It cannot be fully explained or broken down into digestible pieces. I resist any sermon, any teaching that tries to give me a formula for successful prayer.

Is an infant's cry diagrammed for success? Doesn't a mother's milk let down at the mere sound of her child's cry? The child of God prays and the Father's compassion gushes forth. David the psalmist prayed:

> I will call on you, O God,
> for you will answer me;
> give ear to me and hear my prayer.
> Show the wonder of your great love,
> you who save by your right hand
> those who take refuge in you
> from their foes.[20]

In my distress I called to the Lord;
I cried to my God for help.
From his temple he heard my voice;
my cry came before him into his ears.[21]

In the morning, O Lord, You hear my voice;
in the morning I lay my requests before you
and wait in expectation.[22]

The Lord has heard my cry for mercy;
the Lord accepts my prayer.[23]

Now I know that the Lord saves His anointed,
He answers him from his holy heaven with the
Saving power of his right hand.[24]

This is the God of the Bible—our Lord who listens, who hears, who answers, who encourages us and accepts our cries for mercy. It is his joy to show us the "wonder of his great love" in response to our prayers.

Humility: The Foundation of Prayer

Teresa of Avila was a sixteenth-century woman of noble birth who devoted her life to prayer and service to Jesus Christ. For four hundred years her writings have led Christians into deeper understanding of prayer. She wrote, "The whole foundation of prayer must be laid in humility."[25]

Old Testament saints, humbled before the holiness of God, worshiped him and confessed their sin, bringing him the sacrifice of a pure, spotless animal in anticipation of the Lamb of God who would take away the sin of the world.

Today, we come to God aware of our sin, clinging to the cross where that Lamb was slain. Humbled by our filth, we cry out for cleansing. Then, scrubbed clean, we stand, humbled again by the great condescension of our God whose gentleness makes us great.[26]

Always, we begin with the knowledge of our unworthiness. Then we move into the joy of "tender acceptance," as Brennan Manning described it. And our prayers find welcome in the ears of God.

"Yelps of naked need"[27] at times, our prayers often are inarticulate cries, but God hears. We pray "not with the noise of words but with longing."[28] God answers. God responds.

And always we must remember that "not on the strong or the fervent feeling with which I pray does the blessing of the closet depend, but upon the love and power of the Father to whom I there [in the closet of prayer] entrust my needs."[29]

What Matters Most

"Prayer is nothing else than being on terms of friendship with God. It is frequently conversing in secret with Him who loves us," wrote Teresa of Avila.[30]

Walter Wangerin Jr. wrote:

> God is alive. He participates in conversation. His yearning is to be heard, as well as to hear, to lead, to explain, to console, to solve and resolve not only our problems but our very selves, to satisfy not only the petty hungers we can name, but the deeper hungers only a Holy Father can identify.[31]

How easy it is to think only of our requests and shape our prayers carefully, forgetting that the one we are speaking with is a *person*, not a factory for granting wishes. He invites us to pray so we will engage him in conversation, and through conversation, get to know him.

Philip Yancey wrote, "What matters most to God in prayer, I am convinced, is my longing to know Him."[32]

For many of us disciples-in-making, this discovery comes late. In the early days of our spiritual experience, we are told we should pray. We are taught certain elements that are always present in a "good" prayer, and so we learn to include petition, praise, worship, confession, and intercession in our prayers. Each of these elements is good, valuable, and scriptural. But how easily our prayers become rote.

We view prayer as something Christians are supposed to do. As travel agents book cruises, and teachers make lesson plans, so Christians pray.

But if prayer is a task, then the cry of a baby for its mother's arms is mere duty; a lover's whisper is little more than a job well done.

The Only Guarantees

My friend Connie decided to pray the prayer of Jabez. "Enlarge my borders, Lord," she prayed, asking for the blessing Jabez received.

She waited.

She continued to pray.

God's answer surprised her. He brought two crotchety old men into her home—they had no place else to go, so Connie and her husband, Jim, enlarged their borders to make room for them.

"They were both destitute," she said. One was a cousin with no other source of help, the other a friend of a friend in desperate need of a bed and meals for a few weeks. Connie and Jim fixed up a small room by the garage and a friend brought over an extra coffeepot so the men could make their own morning brew.

"I thought I said, 'Enlarge my borders,'" Connie said, "but maybe I said 'boarders.'"

It wasn't what Connie asked for. But it was what God was pleased to give her.

This is a hard lesson in prayer for most of us. We read the Bible's invitation to pray. We see Jesus' words to "ask me for anything in my name, and I will do it."[33] And then it seems he does things we don't like. Or he doesn't do the things we're asking. We hear preachers tell us to "name it and claim it," and still our family members get sick and die. Our friends get divorced. Our children move away. Our jobs change, we are displaced and discouraged. And we wonder what it means to pray.

"Ask, and it shall be given you,"[34] we read.

We're asking. It seems we're not getting.

"This is one of the greatest mysteries of the Christian life," said my friend, author Alan Elliott. His wife, Annette, died recently from a malignant brain tumor. "God instructs us to ask, seek, and find, but our understanding of what that means is still clouded by ignorance of his power and wisdom. We usually only see life from this side of eternity and are mostly concerned about the problems we have today. But he sees our lives in a much larger context and deals with us with that knowledge."

In some situations, it's a matter of obvious, blatant sin. We've asked amiss, in order to satisfy our lust for power, or prestige, or so that we may enjoy luxuries never promised.[35] Sometimes we ask out of confusion, out of fear. We are "double-minded,"[36] uncertain that we really want God's will, unconvinced that his ways are best. Yet, even in such circumstances, God often surprises us with grace. He grants a miracle of healing or mercy, although we are filthy in our sin.

"Frankly, I've seen God astound a 'sinner' with a miracle while a saint struggles—on the surface—with no answer at all," Alan said. Is it any wonder that confusion often accompanies our prayer life?

But the confusion begins to lift a bit when we grasp this truth: the only guarantees God gives are the eternal, invisible ones.

God absolutely guarantees that he will give us what we need, not necessarily what we've asked for.[37]

God promises wisdom to his children who ask for it.[38]

God promises forgiveness of sin, when we ask on the basis of Jesus' sacrificial death.[39]

God promises to stand alongside us, to strengthen us and uphold us and never forsake us.[40]

God promises to work all things together for our good if we are his children.[41]

God promises everlasting life for those who have put their whole trust in Christ.[42]

The promises of God are numerous, and precious. But they do not include relief from suffering, exemption from hard times, or freedom from stress and duress.

The simple act of praying does not ensure us financial prosperity or success in every endeavor. It does not inoculate us against cruel people and harsh circumstances. We can look at the disciples and see that even they were not spared hardships. Nor was our Lord himself, even though he prayed with passion and purity that the most holy among us will never be able to fully emulate.

The apostle Paul is an example of one who prayed faithfully, in the power of the Holy Spirit, and yet still endured the worst that life could throw at him.

Today we can look at the most saintly among us and see that their godliness, their lives of prayer do not insulate them against the human experience. Yet prayer does bring God's sovereignty and transcendence into every experience.

Through prayer, we are able to go through life actively involved with a loving God, the Lord who names himself *El-Shaddai*—the God who is enough.

At its most basic expression, prayer is not a wish list but a relationship. If I am coming to God only to get what I want, only to get what I think I need, I am missing the purpose and significance of prayer.

How often we pass over this essential point: the heart of God is at the heart of prayer. This may be why ancient Christian writers so often coupled the mention of prayer with meditation. Meditation warms our hearts toward God, alerts us to his loving presence, enables us to see him as a person who longs to hear our voices of love, who desires to speak with us and to us. It prevents us from cheapening the relationship with our Father by marching into the throne room of God and immediately whipping out a shopping list of needs and desires.

As a father himself, my husband can identify with that scenario. There were times in our family when he asked me, "Do you see a big sign on my chest that says *ATM*?" Our kids were in college, and at times communication was infrequent unless they needed money. It wasn't that we didn't want to give them what they needed, but we missed them. We missed being part of their lives, their laughter and companionship. We felt diminished by their dismissal of us as little more than money machines.

We must never come to God with the idea that we can push a few buttons, enter a PIN—using the name of Jesus as a sort of code word to get the Father's approval—and then wait while he doles out whatever we've asked for.

Calvin Miller put it this way: "To desire only what Christ gives and not to desire Christ Himself is to be bought off by little trinkets, never to own the greater treasure of His indwelling presence."[43]

Prayer is more than making requests, although we are told to come boldly to the throne of grace.[44]

It is more than asking, although we are told to ask.[45]

Prayer is not just a time we use to communicate our needs and desires to God, although we are told to bring him our requests.[46]

Our great need, wrote Eugene Peterson, is "not communication but communion."[47]

Through prayer we commune with God; we align ourselves with his purposes. We learn the sound of his voice. We discover his power and learn to trust his promises.

We learn to rest in the reality that his ways are not our ways. We learn to submit to God's greater wisdom and knowledge. "Some humble grow at last, and still, / And then God gives them what they will."[48]

A Time and Place

Connie's "boarders" don't like to make their own coffee. They like to come into the house where Connie's husband has an office, where Connie has long-established morning routines. Their presence is taking some adjustment.

For years, Connie has taken her coffee and gone to sit in a

certain chair where she reads her Bible and prays. Next to her chair she keeps a basket with note cards, pens, books she's studying—it's like her devotional/prayer garden. But lately, she's come downstairs to find her cousin sitting in her chair, sipping coffee from the pot in her kitchen.

"I've had to move upstairs," Connie said. "And it's so difficult—it doesn't feel right. It's as if God is still downstairs!"

I understand how Connie feels. For years, I've had a special place where I go alone to meet God and pray. When guests in the house or some unexpected events interrupt my routine, I feel jarred, off center. I have to quickly regroup and find another place and time to pray in private.

In the early years of my faith, legalism might have been a reason for my feelings of disruption. I would have felt as though God was unhappy with me, as though I had somehow failed by not having prayed alone for a specific period of time. I would have been waiting, watching for God to "zap" me.

But as I have grown in my understanding of God's unconditional love for me, I have come to value my time with him as one does a special date with an intimate friend. If circumstances get in the way of my private time with God, I can't wait to make time later in my day to be alone with him, to listen to him, talk to him, without distractions, without interruptions.

I feel lonely for him, not guilty—unless a rebellious attitude is keeping me away. In those instances, God is teaching me to come running to him quickly for forgiveness, even if my heart hasn't quite finished enjoying my sin.

Teresa of Avila's words comfort and encourage me: "He gives the wandering soul the desire to pray on, even when it has not yet left off all sin."[49]

Jesus' Prayer Life

Jesus' prayer life while he was on earth showed us the deep longing he had for his Father. Many times in the Gospels we see him going to a solitary place to pray while it is still early, still dark outside.

Of all the things the disciples watched Jesus do, prayer was the one thing that prompted them to ask, "Teach us how to do that."[50]

I wonder if I had been among their number, if I might have asked for instructions on how to heal. "Teach me that, Lord," I'd have said. Or "Show me how to feed a crowd with a loaf of bread and a can of tuna, and have leftovers for a week, Lord. Give me the words to say to make that happen."

But the people closest to Jesus observed his prayer life. Startling, powerful, his prayers reflected an intimacy and communion with God that they had never experienced. "Show us how to draw near to Yahweh like that," they asked. "Teach us to commune with God the way you do."

I could imagine Peter, James, and John, the fishermen, asking Jesus to grant them power over the winds and the seas; and it is no stretch to think Luke the doctor might have asked for power to heal. It would have been understandable if Matthew the taxman had asked Jesus to show him how to pull a coin out of the mouth of a fish. But those who knew him best did not ask for greater power so they could succeed in business, nor for power they could wield in human relationships. They asked for power in prayer, for intimacy with God.

And so Jesus taught them these principles in Matthew 6:

Come to God on the basis of relationship, nothing else—call him Father.

Come to God in humility. Recognize his holiness, his majesty, his sovereign rule and power over all things.

Ask him for the things you need today, trusting him for tomorrow's needs tomorrow.

Seek forgiveness, and extend it to others. Understand that by withholding it, when you have the power to give it, you rob yourself of the very forgiveness you seek from God.

Ask for protection from evil, for God to shield you from temptation that would overpower you.

Exclaim the greatness of God, worship him. Adore him. Pursue his glory above all things.

The Lord's Prayer covered all the exigencies of human life as Christ experienced it. Even the matter of forgiveness was relevant; although Jesus had no need to ask for forgiveness himself, the opportunities for him to exercise forgiveness on a daily basis were many.

Our pattern for prayer comes from Jesus' heart. He who told us to be humble humbled himself, although he was equal with God; he trusted himself to the Father's sovereignty— "Nevertheless not my will but thine be done"; he sought the power of God during temptation; he adored his Father and proclaimed his lavish love for him. In the final moments of his life, Jesus committed his spirit into the hands of his Father with utter trust.

Make no mistake: the men and women who traveled with Jesus, who housed him, fed him, ate with him, and anointed his head with perfume, those who listened to his words and watched his miraculous works, wanted this one thing: to know the Father the way Jesus knew the Father.

Today, as his disciples, we can desire nothing more valuable, nothing more essential.

Tuesdays with Margaret

My friend Margaret and I meet weekly to pray. Praying aloud has always been hard for me. As a child, I often felt I had to pray on command—say something, sound spiritual, add a quick "amen." Over the years I've avoided praying in groups unless I couldn't escape. I pray with Ken, but I prefer to listen to him. Most of my out-loud prayers are the ones I prayed with my children at bedtime. So, praying with Margaret, in the beginning, was a stretch for me, but I felt God was encouraging me to do it.

Praying with Margaret was one way I could show my friendship and love for her while she was engaged with her husband John in the battle against Lou Gehrig's disease. No matter how alone and frightened she might be throughout the week, she could know that on Tuesday afternoons she was not alone with her heartbreak. We would be together. We would be praying.

I never imagined how much Margaret would minister to me. We pray over lists—adding new names and situations every week. Sometimes we go back a few pages and write the specific answers to prayer we've seen. We pray for John, the treatments; for medical research and advancement against ALS. We pray for healing, for a miracle.

But we pray for ourselves too, that we will have generous, loving hearts. We pray for our children, their friends, their spouses, their jobs, their spiritual lives. We pray for our church, our parents, our friends, and their hurts.

Recently, we sat for more than an hour and talked about all God had done in response to our prayers. Not every answer was a yes, but every answer was from the throne of grace. We couldn't doubt the work of God in the circumstances we had entrusted to him. In some instances we saw how God had changed our

requests, transformed our desires, and then given us things that
we didn't know we wanted until he placed them in our hands.

With Margaret, I've seen grace personified. Often I am awed
by her prayers. Sometimes when we are together, John is at home
hooked up to an IV, undergoing a treatment that won't save his
life but will enable him to have greater strength for a while—no
one knows how long. I listen to Margaret pray for my daughter in
law school, that she will pass her exams. I listen to her ask God
to bless my writing efforts, to protect my husband as he travels, to
give me peace and wisdom to deal with a difficult person in my
life. Margaret, in her prayers for me, models the suffering Christ
who bore our burdens. She humbles me.

She begins with praise, often praying Psalms. I listen, thinking of all that is breaking her heart, and I hear her worship God,
thanking him for Jesus, for access to the Father, for his great and
unfathomable plan for her life. She praises him for the beauty of
the flowers, the music of the birds, the pleasure of my friendship.
She adores the Father and trusts him utterly. Every request she
mentions boldly, then quickly leaves all to the kind and loving
will of God.

I've read books on prayer, done Bible studies on prayer, and
listened to prayers all my life. But praying with Margaret has
taught me more about prayer than anything I've ever studied.

I've learned the beautiful truth that God is very present
when two or three get together in his name. I've learned that
God is pleased to give us the desires of our hearts, if at times he
must change our hearts first.

Together we often talk about what God is doing, and not
doing, in response to our prayers. We've learned that what
Eugene Peterson said is true: "Instead of asking why the help has
not come, the person at prayer learns to look carefully at what is

actually going on in her life . . . and ask, 'Could *this* be the help that He is providing? I never thought of *this* in terms of help, but maybe it is.'"[51]

Praying with Margaret has taught me that love for God grows through prayer. And friendship with his children grows in the same way.

I've learned that there is nothing too small, too insignificant to pray about.

Mostly, I've learned that "it is not a vain thing to trust in the Living God."[52]

Pray Without Ceasing

When Margaret and I say good-bye on Tuesday afternoons, our praying doesn't end.

Christians' whole lives are one long prayer. It begins with that first "yelp" when we call on God for mercy and claim the death of Christ as the payment for our sins. It doesn't end until prayer becomes a face-to-face conversation with Jesus in heaven.

From start to finish, the life of faith is one continuous conversation with God. We share our hearts with him, we listen to his; we worship, praise, adore; we ask, seek, cry, repent. It never ends—this ongoing communion with the Lord who lives in us through his Holy Spirit. Nothing can separate us from his love through Christ Jesus.

"Amen" is not the end, like a period placed at the end of a sentence. It is a word of agreement with God. We pray, we say, "So be it," and then we continue on. Through it all, through every conversation, God makes himself available to us. All his resources are ours, all his compassion is ours, all his tenderness, his power, his joy, his gladness. Prayer teaches us to delight in his sufficiency. It teaches us that God can be trusted.

George Müller was a man of prayer. When he died in 1898 at the age of ninety-three, he had served God for nearly seventy years, founding orphanages throughout England, caring for thousands of children, and preaching in forty-two countries. His testimony, though yellowed with age, is timely for us still.

"The joy that answers to prayer give cannot be described," he wrote, "and the impetus that they afford to the spiritual life is exceedingly great."[53]

God makes himself known to us through prayer. He reveals his heart, responds to our neediness, conveys his love, and communes with us through prayer. Is it any wonder that great saints through the centuries have upheld prayer as a vital discipline of our faith?

Prayer is "our only safety!" cried Fénelon;[54] "our whole service to God," preached John Donne.[55]

Prayer, for all of us, is all those things. It is the essence of the life of faith.

Here is a startling truth: God collects our prayers! Like a husband who refuses to part with love letters from his bride, God keeps all our prayers, saving them, storing them in "golden bowls."[56] Throughout eternity, the prayers of his beloved will be preserved, like pages from a lover's diary, in a never-ending tribute to the "sacred romance."[57]

Jesus Is Still Praying—for Us!

I missed a prayer session at a conference once, and I was devastated. "Emele prayed for us," a woman told me, and I knew something special had occurred without me.

The daughter of a former headhunter from the island of Fiji, Emele was profoundly converted when the gospel penetrated her village. Her whole family accepted the good news, and she and all her brothers and sisters became messengers to the world of the transforming power of Jesus Christ.

To listen to Emele pray heats up your heart and makes your spirit ache for God. I couldn't believe I had missed the experience of having her pray for me, personally, specifically. Imagine the power, the blessing!

And then Jesus whispered in my soul, "Jan, I'm praying for you." How casually I take that fact: that Jesus is at this moment sitting at the right hand of the Father, communing with him, making requests on my behalf, interceding for me.[58] Is there anything he would ask for me that the Father would deny him?

"He who did not spare his own Son, but gave him up for us all—how will he not also, along with him, graciously give us all things?"[59]

I love how John Piper explained this verse: "God did not spare His own Son! How much more then will He spare no effort to give me all that Christ died to purchase—all things, all good. It is as sure as the certainty that He loved His own Son."[60]

Piper also wrote:

God desired two things: *not* to see His Son made a mockery by sinners; and not to see His people denied infinite future grace. Surely it is more likely that He will spare His Son than that He will spare us. But no. He did not spare His Son. And therefore it is impossible that He should spare us the promise for which the Son died—He will freely with Him give us all things.

. . . Giving us all things is the easy thing. . . . The hard part is already done [handing over his Son to ridicule and torture]. But He did it. And now all future grace is not only sure; it is easy.[61]

Jesus, in perfect sync with the will of the Father, knows me intimately, perfectly. He will never ask "amiss." He will always be my advocate, my intercessor, my prayer partner. And the Father will always hear him and answer with a resounding "Yes!"

The Mark of True Believers

"The Christ-desire is the mark of a real believer," wrote Calvin Miller.[62] Prayer and meditation, working together, feed that desire. Meditation focuses our hearts on Christ, the Bridegroom, and the love that sent him in pursuit of us. It enables us to envision the creative power of God at work on our behalf; it gives us hope and confidence to trust. Prayer brings us into his presence, where his arms encircle us, his voice is heard, and his heartbeat is felt.

Prayer and meditation show us the beauty of God. For he *is* beautiful!

> And the life that expresses His glory should be beautiful. . . . Beauty and truth do not come by mystical revelation and inspiration in a moment of motionless mental waiting. Beauty and truth come by painstaking thinking [meditation!] and trial and praying and self-correcting.[63]

This is why they are called "disciplines."

*   *   *

The doctor called with the news of the biopsy. The growth was benign. I breathed a deep sigh of relief and thanked God.

This time, I thought. *But next time, who knows?* "Lord, make me strong to meet whatever lies ahead for me," I prayed.

I determined to stay on my knees, even though the crisis had passed. I committed before God to keep the communion fresh and sweet between my Lord and me, even when times are smooth, easy. I can't forget Jeremiah the prophet's warning: "If you stumble in safe country, / how will you manage in the thickets / by the Jordan?"[64]

The apostle's words echo: pray without ceasing.

9

~

LOVE IN ACTION

THE DISCIPLINE OF SERVICE

*O*n September 11, 2001, I watched in horror with millions of Americans as flames engulfed the World Trade Center towers. Moments later, still stunned, I saw them sink into the ground as melted steel girders folded and the towers dissolved into a hideous gray cloud. I saw the gaping wound in the side of the Pentagon and watched fire and smoke rise in terrifying plumes from a farmer's field in Pennsylvania.

In the hours and days that followed, men and women hurled themselves into service for their neighbors, their countrymen. While firemen and trained rescue teams searched the rubble for survivors, others, ordinary citizens—stockbrokers, sanitation workers, cab drivers, steelworkers—joined the effort, forming a human conveyor belt to haul and sift debris in search of clues, personal effects, anything that might aid in the investigation of the crime or the identification of victims. Men and women around the country waited in block-long lines to give blood.

New York streets filled with people handing sandwiches and

water bottles to rescue workers. At one point, messages crawled across television screens saying, "Enough! We've got enough food and water for the rescuers."

We were a nation in action, serving our friends, our family, our fellow citizens. Against an ugly backdrop of unspeakable evil, it was a scene of transcendent beauty.

I was studying the discipline of service during those days, trying to structure a chapter that would bring meaning and clarity to Christian women who are busy, already active in many kinds of service. I was suddenly overwhelmed. Everywhere I looked people were serving, many of whom may not have had any kind of "religious experience," many of whom may not consider themselves Christian.

What could I say about the service of so many diverse people who so quickly and willingly rush to the aid of strangers? What could I say about service that bloodies our clothes, burns our eyes, and fills our nostrils with choking dust?

It occurred to me that never is God more visible in the world than when his creatures are engaged in service to others.

"Let us make man in our image, in our likeness," God said.[1] This is the God who reveals himself in the metaphor of a Shepherd. This is the God who is a Gardener, a Father. All these titles describe one who cares, tends, leads, serves, and ministers to the needs of those who are weaker, those who are in need. He is the Father to the child, the Shepherd to the sheep, the Farmer to his vines.

The God revealed in the Bible serves continually, without need for rest; never depleted, never weary. The very concept of service emanates from his heart. It is an evidence of his imprint on his creation that we respond to needs with an urgency to serve. It is a visible tribute to the greatness of our invisible God that the pain of others touches us, that we are inclined to step into chaos and catastrophes to offer succor and safety.

Only men and women hardened against the reality of grace can withhold such service. Only the most depraved and deluded can despise and reject the vision of the image of God in others.

On that horrid September day we saw the work of individuals so deluded, so blinded by hatred that they could kill and destroy without remorse. But we also saw the evidence of God's grace. We saw it in the actions of thousands of Americans who responded to urgent needs with heroic service.

We saw it in hundreds of countries all around the world as men and women observed a moment of prayer in honor of America's suffering. In Albania, the only country in the world to have officially declared itself an atheistic state, thousands of citizens filled the capital city, responding to the prime minister's request that all Albanians pause for three minutes to pray for America.

The imprint of God has indelibly marked his creation. In New York, amid the rubble and the danger and the horrific trauma, men and women served in those critical hours and days because it was right. It was good. All around us, day and night, amid the disastrous as well as the mundane, men and women in countries both Christian and non-Christian choose to serve humanity because it is right. It is good.

What then needs to be said about service?

If service emerges from us, a flawed yet powerful exhibit of the tattered image of God still present in his damaged creation, how then is it a discipline? If those who claim no faith serve alongside those of faith, how is service a spiritual discipline?

Dallas Willard wrote that some serving is "simply an act of love and righteousness"[2]—of which any individual is capable. Regardless of one's relationship to God, the very presence of common grace in our world gives us some knowledge, some idea, albeit limited, of what love and righteousness look like.

Jesus, in his conversations with individuals during his earthly incarnation, often alluded to their righteous acts. He acknowledged their love of their families. He never suggested that men and women don't know how to love or perform kind acts and good deeds.

As he preached on the mountainside, thousands heard him say, "If you, being sinful, know how to give good gifts, imagine what kind of gifts your perfect, holy heavenly Father gives!"

The inference is clear: even in our fallen state we do know how to give good gifts; we do know how to do good deeds; we do know how to love.

By that statement Jesus affirmed that the human heart, created by God and stamped with his image, has the ability to do good deeds, to love others, and to serve. The capacity to serve, then, is universal.

What then, for the Christian, is service?

Is it rallying to a cause?

Is it always "good"? Or is it possible to pervert service, turning it into leverage for future gain and benefits?

Is service accomplished only when we have invested ourselves in others?

What constitutes the spiritual discipline of service?

For the redeemed individual, saved by faith in Jesus Christ, service becomes a discipline when I "serve another to train myself away from arrogance, possessiveness, envy, resentment, or covetousness."[3]

When my service is not necessarily blatantly patriotic, when my service is hidden, when serving asks me to do things that my culture does not applaud, things my nature is not attracted to, I am exercising the discipline of service.

When I deliberately choose to pursue servanthood as an identity, a lifestyle, rather than celebrity, when I reject the lure of power and entitlement in favor of service, I am exercising the discipline of service.

Picking Up the Towel

Clear away the smoke and debris from the site of a catastrophe and most of those who served return to lives as account executives, restaurateurs, librarians, teachers, sales managers, homemakers, counselors, doctors. Service was what we did for a moment, an hour, maybe longer. But it is not what defines us. We hand out business cards to do that.

Having served, we would not call ourselves servants.

But that is exactly what Jesus called himself. And it is exactly what the discipline of service requires us to do: identify ourselves, not as business professionals, or medical technicians, or homemakers, or any other label that describes what we *do*, but rather to accept for ourselves an identity, a label that defines who and what we *are* in Christ.

> Now that I, your Lord and Teacher, have washed your feet, you also should wash one another's feet. I have set you an example that you should do as I have done for you. I tell you the truth, no servant is greater than his master, nor is a messenger greater than the one who sent him. Now that you know these things, you will be blessed if you do them.[4]

Elijah handed his mantle to Elisha, giving him the authority and identity of a prophet. Jesus, rising up from the floor, his hands dripping with dirty water, handed his disciples a towel.

"This will be your banner," he was saying. "This will identify you as servants."

If they were hoping for a scepter, or a sword, they were disappointed. "The basin will be your way to blessing," he promised. "Be servants in a world that values celebrity."

His meaning was clear: "As my disciples, you are to be people who resist the very human yearnings for applause, for approval, for ease and pleasant circumstances in order to perform the lowly, unseen, and unrewarded acts of service. You are to be people who don't insist on ascending the dais to the sound of applause. You are to be people who choose to descend to your knees with a basin and a towel."

They were hard words then. They are hard words now.

Our world is no different today from what it was two thousand years ago when Jesus' followers bickered over their status, wanting to be assured of positions of honor in his kingdom. Servanthood is not and never has been a popular career choice.

While we may enjoy performing certain acts of service, we have little desire to be described as servants; we much prefer to be known as celebrities. Yet Jesus, the King of kings, who deserved all the perks of celebrity, all the accoutrements of royalty, turned his back on all that heaven offered and became a servant in order to express love in actions that we could understand.

His works seldom met with applause. He knelt in the dirt to mix mud from spit. He handled common bread and filleted fish for meals. He walked miles out of his way to share a drink of water with a disreputable woman. On any given day, he could be found mingling with outcasts, eating meals with crooks, explaining eternal truth to slow-witted fishermen, and rescuing the demon-possessed. His was not glamorous work.

As Jesus' disciples, serious about following him, we may need to adjust our notions about service to match his. We will have to answer the question: Am I willing to be "banished to the mundane, the ordinary, the trivial,"[5] if the Father asks it of me?

If we are uncomfortable with towels and basins and the thought of serving in lowly ways and in grubby places, where there is no applause and no television camera, we haven't yet grasped the divine concept of servanthood. We have failed to comprehend that "the Lord walks among the pots and pans."[6]

Motives for Service

Willingness to serve in lowly settings and perform unlovely tasks—this is not the only measure of true servanthood. A neighbor illustrated that for me many years ago. The lesson echoes still.

"She owes me. I took care of her kids twice last week. I can call her and ask her to baby-sit mine and she'll have to say yes."

The comment stunned me. I had thought my neighbor had a generous servant's heart. She was always offering to take my son along with her when she ran errands or took her children to the park—"just to give you a little break, Jan," she would say as she loaded my toddler into her car.

I thought she was crazy even if kind. She had two children of her own, but she'd say, "What's one more?" And so she would trundle off, three car seats buckled in her Volvo station wagon.

One day, after she'd taken another neighbor's brood with her, she told me, "Oh, I plan these little trips. Taking a bunch to the park is easy. I just sit and watch them run around for a little while, then put them back in the car and hand them a treat for the ride home. Sherri is so grateful. She won't be able to say no when I ask her to keep mine next week—she'll have to feed them lunch and put them down for a nap. I'm getting the best of this deal."

I made a mental note to decline the next time this neighbor offered to "give me a break." And I vowed never to forget that living metaphor of what service is not.

Service is *not* a leverage tool for prying something out of others in order to serve ourselves.

It is *not* a means by which we bank purchasing power for our own comfort and convenience at a later time.

Jesus made it clear: we can't serve God and selfish purposes, selfish gains, at the same time.[7]

I've not met many people as blatant and unashamed of their motives as my neighbor. But all of us are tempted to serve for the wrong reasons. Our motives may vary, but if they focus on how we can gain something for ourselves or how we can obligate others, we haven't served our neighbor; we have indentured her.

Service Never Stands Alone

Service, as a spiritual discipline, is intricately connected with the other disciplines.

The psalmist told us to serve the Lord with gladness[8]—celebration takes its place beside service.

Serve in secret, Jesus said.[9]

Serve with humility, Peter told us.[10]

Sacrifice is service, Paul wrote in Romans.[11]

Prayer is service, the Epistles teach.[12]

It is a dangerous thing to try to exercise the discipline of service (or any of the spiritual disciplines) apart from the exercise of the others. The congregation at the Holy Tabernacle Church of Jesus

Christ Apostolic discovered this painful truth one recent summer.

"Church Members Upset by Tithing Ultimatum"—the small caption in the newspaper caught my eye. The article took my breath away.

It seems that more than two hundred parishioners received a letter from the executive secretary of the church telling them their tithes were in arrears, and that they were in danger of having all their membership privileges revoked if they didn't send in all back tithes within thirty days. (Payments could be made by check or money order.)

"My spirit just kind of broke," said one stunned church member.[13]

Imagine how God's Spirit felt.

When Christians try to pry a spiritual discipline out of one another, all expression of the nature of God is lost. Intimacy with God dissipates. Whatever action results cannot be called service. It is slavery.

The "service" rendered is robbed of celebration. It cannot be considered worship—its goal is not the adoration of God but rather the pleasing of manipulative tyrants. It is unlikely to be accompanied by prayer because the power of human leadership has usurped the authority of God. It is unlikely to be exercised with humility but rather with resentment and fear. It is more ransom than sacrifice: approval and acceptance are its hostages.

Service, to be truly a spiritual discipline, cannot be coerced from us, nor can we coerce it out of others. It cannot be cut off from the exercise of humility, or isolated from secrecy or celebration or worship. The disciplines, like threads woven in a tapestry, give us a portrait of the character of God. To rip out one thread is to alter the portrait and destroy the beauty of his image.

Love's Promise

"We ought not to be weary in doing little things for the love of God. For God does not regard the greatness of the work, but the love with which it is performed," wrote Brother Lawrence.[14]

Any discussion of service always circles back to a discussion of love. And the beauty of love is this: it always succeeds. Its goal is its beginning; its end is its means. In the first moment that love is expressed, its success is ensured.

If the members of the Holy Tabernacle Church yielded to threats and coercion and wrote out their tithe checks under duress, the church's ledgers may have thrived, but the church itself would have been a failure.

"If I speak in the tongues of men and of angels, but have not love, I am only a resounding gong or a clanging cymbal. . . . If I give all I possess to the poor and surrender my body to the flames, but have not love, I gain nothing."[15] Preaching and giving are two vital acts of service in the minds of most Christians, yet God considers them obnoxious and worthless if we do not carry them out with love.

Service, in the broadest sense, is putting our love for God into action. It is remembering that "the Lord doesn't look so much at the greatness of our works [as in collecting large amounts of money for operating a church] as at the love with which they are done."[16]

Priorities in Service

"My mom's not home," the teenage girl said. "Can I talk to you?"

My friend answered, "Of course, sweetie. But where's your mom?"

"She's working at the soup kitchen."

This wasn't just a one-time occurrence. The teenager called often, looking for a woman who would listen and care. She was hungry for the love and companionship that her mother was serving up to strangers at a downtown soup kitchen.

How easy it is to squander our service in generic giving and miss the obvious needs of those in our own family. Dick Hillis said it well, I think: "Love best those closest to you."

The founder of O.C. International, he was addressing a group of about three hundred missionaries, young families as well as veterans. They all had gathered at the mission headquarters in Colorado Springs to honor him and celebrate his sixty years of missionary service. I was invited as his biographer.

Sitting in the back of the room, listening to Dr. Hillis, I sensed he had chosen his words carefully. For the next several minutes, he urged his audience to prioritize in their ministry. "Don't forget your own children in your urgency to save the world," he was saying. "Don't sacrifice your husband, your wife, your family, in the effort to serve others."

He had seen it too many times—angry, rebellious children of missionaries and pastors, deacons and elders, kids who had been shoved aside all their lives so that someone else's children could be served; spouses neglected while the families of others were nurtured in the name of Christianity.

It happens in all kinds of families.

Eugene Peterson warns us that Paul's New Testament teachings "will not permit us to compensate for neglecting those nearest us by advertising our compassion for those on another continent. . . . The check for the starving child must still be written and the missionary sent, but as an *extension* of what we are doing at home, not as an *exemption* from it."[17]

Dr. John Friel and Linda Friel wrote: "Putting as much energy into being with and helping people we hardly know as we put into our close relationships can be okay; but only if our own house is in order. Many of us take care of the entire world while our own feelings and our children and spouses are hurt, empty, lonely and wounded. We must take care of *first things first.*"[18]

"First things first" includes caring for the urgent needs of our own souls, our own bodies, because "a life that is totally focused on others will disintegrate. . . . We need to care with a care that springs from being nurtured ourselves."[19]

"Love your neighbor as yourself," God commanded.[20] Sometimes it's a good idea to ask: Would my neighbors have reason to be afraid of me if I loved them the way I love myself?

We need reminders that our service should extend beyond ourselves and our families only after we have adequately, appropriately addressed those needs in love. Paul made that clear in his instructions to the young pastor, Timothy: "If anyone does not provide for his relatives, especially his immediate family, he has denied the faith and is worse than an unbeliever."[21]

My mother- and father-in-law have long served God by arranging worship services and doing visitation in several nursing homes in their community. Over the years, they have forged loving friendships with many of the sick and elderly who are lonely and in desperate need of kindness. My father-in-law's diagnosis of cancer interrupted their work. In the months before his death, my mother-in-law said, "I miss the ministry, but right now my priority is Papa."

Others stepped in to carry on in the nursing homes. Mom chose to serve best that one closest to her: her husband. She won't receive a trophy for it, as she did last year. The local newspaper isn't likely to write a feature story about her again, but she served in the name of Jesus Christ.

Brennan Manning wrote, "We define ourselves by our response to human need."[22] Perhaps it is our response to the needs of those closest to us that define us most clearly.

Turning Work into Rest

Jesus said, "Are you tired? Worn out? Burned out on religion? Come to me. Get away with me and you'll recover your life. I'll show you how to take a real rest. Walk with me and work with me—watch how I do it. Learn the unforced rhythms of grace."[23]

Grace pulses faithfully, but often we miss its tempo because we are listening to other rhythms. Ego sets a pounding pace and fear can beat a furious tempo. Our movements become forced, unsteady, impulse-driven. We grow weary in service, wondering if there is any point; wondering if anyone cares.

"Watch how I do it," Jesus told us. "Walk with me. Work with me."

The "unforced rhythms of grace" pulsed along the dirty roads of Galilee, through the cities, into the synagogues. The heartbeat of God pounded wherever Jesus walked. He didn't have to strive to serve. Service occurred in his every encounter. It was a river pouring out of his divine nature: spontaneous, unforced, at times unplanned, but always in sync with his Father's will. This is important for us to know.

Of course, we will serve in association with an organization, a civic group, a specific church initiative. That's fine. But most of the service we render will occur in the course of normal activity.

Wherever we go, indwelled by God's Spirit, we take the power and glory of the kingdom of God. He allows us to be his vessels for infusing transcendence into the ordinary, glory into the mundane, and significance into the trivial.

The unforced rhythms of grace are these: ordinary tasks, required at the moment, permeated with glory because they are done in the name of Jesus.

Fénelon wrote, "We cannot be doing great things all the time, but we can do the things that are suitable to our condition in life. We are already doing a great deal if we hold our tongues, suffer, and pray when we cannot do something outwardly."[24]

To Know Ourselves Safe

I signed up as a parent-volunteer for my daughter's eighth-grade wilderness trip only because Molly said she wanted me to go. A parents' meeting the week before the trip confirmed my worst fears: we would sleep outside in tents, cook our own food, wash in the river, and generally do scary things like spelunking, canoeing, rock climbing, and belaying.

Most of the week I spent vacillating between sheer terror and absolute bliss. The canoe trip down the Buffalo River was terror—the river was fifteen feet above flood stage, and ours was the first and last team allowed on the river before we were all evacuated from the area to finish our week at a youth encampment in Missouri. Hot showers at the camp were bliss after having washed for three days in frigid river water.

Before we left on this adventure, of course, we were told to expect difficult challenges. We would be doing things we had never done before. There would be an element of danger in many of the activities; we should expect minor scrapes and bumps as there were always a few. But the leaders assured us they were well trained and experienced. They had first-aid kits. They knew the river, the terrain, the rock cliffs, the caves. They would be bringing the best equipment available, and they would show us how to be safe and how to ensure the children's safety.

This information meant a lot to me while I was standing atop an eighty-foot wall, trying to summon the courage to step off backward.

I remembered that experience recently when I read Dorothy Sayers's words about servanthood—that the resurrected Christ empowers us to "do something about the problem of sin and suffering." The disciples "had seen the strong hands of Christ twist the crown of thorns into a crown of glory," she wrote, "and in hands as strong as that they knew themselves safe."[25] We can do unimaginable things when we believe ourselves safe in the power and goodness of God.

As a young woman serving God in India, Amy Carmichael ignored death threats and rescued hundreds of children who had been given to Hindu temples to serve as prostitutes. She dared to serve God in dangerous ways, risking her life. She learned to "tuck herself into God."[26]

Our service may not be so dramatic, but in the power of God we can do those things that seem scary, impossible, unpleasant.

We can care for the unlovely.

We can minister to a dying parent, a suffering friend, or a needy stranger.

We can enter into the adventure of servanthood, following Christ, loving and caring and giving, knowing that he will never fail us or forsake us. He has gone before us; he has prepared the way; he will supply everything we need—the air we breathe, the energy in our muscles, the passion in our souls.

The Grand Adventure

I think Amy Carmichael would say a loud and hearty "amen" to John Eldredge's words: "Where would we be if Jesus was not fierce and wild and romantic to the core?"[27]

How easy it is to lose sight of the magnificent adventure we share with Christ, our Bridegroom, who pursued us to the point of death and then conquered even that in order to redeem us and make us his beloved.

This is the God who calls a woman to the sort of high drama that rescues abandoned children from ancient pagan temples!

This is the God who whispered to my friend Anita, "Come with me!" And for love of him she left her friends, her family, her livelihood, to join him in the adventure of mentoring young women in a Bible school in Albania.

Our vision of Jesus, the Son of God, is too often dull and drab. How we need a fresh view of him—to see him as the mighty God who loves a daring adventure, who has no fear of risk and danger. What was the Incarnation, if not the most daring of risks?

This is the God who calls us to work with him, alongside him, to share in his mission to wrench good out of evil.

Something deep inside me responds to the drama and challenge of serving, of helping in the building of the kingdom of God. I am formed, at heart, as a helpmeet in the image of God. As his bride, his beloved, I'm engaged in his cause, that of demonstrating the kindness and compassion of the Father's heart; that of sharing the good news that the God who loves the world is a Warrior-King who will one day conquer every remaining foe and take his bride home to live with him forever.

Lately, I've begun praying, "Lord, give me a clearer, brighter vision of you as the magnificent God who rejoices over me as a Bridegroom does over his bride."[28] Yes, it is true that Jesus walks among the pots and pans, but he also rides the winds and thunders across mountain peaks.

Rewards of Service

Phoebe was Paul the Apostle's friend. "She's been a great help to me and to many others," he wrote in a letter to the Roman Christians. "I commend her to you."[29]

That is the Bible's only mention of Phoebe. In calling her a servant, Paul used the Greek word *diakonos* or "deacon," which we usually associate with a group of men elected from the congregation to attend to the nitty-gritty details of service within the church. But here, Paul used *diakonos* to describe this godly *woman*, placing her in the ranks with the men he wrote about in 1 Timothy—men he described as having authentic faith and being worthy of respect. In Hebrews, the writer said this of such servants: God "will not forget your work and the love you have shown him as you have helped his people and continue to help them."[30]

Paul added this word: "Those who have served well gain an excellent standing and great assurance in their faith in Christ Jesus."[31]

Here's what that means: the woman who willingly takes on the identity of a servant, in the name of Jesus, is not stepping down, though our culture might view it in that light. In the eyes of God, she is stepping up. And the result, for her, will be a surging increase in the level of confidence she has in God and an ever-increasing boldness in her faith.

It is as Jesus said: the basin is the way of blessing.

*   *   *

On September 11, 2001, our hearts were hideously scarred, as were New York's skyline, the walls of the Pentagon, and a field in Pennsylvania. But within days, President Bush urged us to refuse to let this evil destroy us. "Resume your lives," he said. "Get back to the business of living."

Amid a new normalcy, we have gone back to our jobs, our travel schedules, our hobbies. We have resumed the habit of handing out business cards that define us, cards that say *Realtor, Vice President of Sales*, or *Attorney-at-Law*. But the Christian's business of living requires that our hearts be boldly embossed with the word *Servant*.

Our business of living means being an exhibit of the character of God, a display of his kingdom, a witness to his purposes. Our business of living remains that of being a servant. It means preaching the good news; it means binding up the brokenhearted, comforting the mourners, replacing ashes with the oil of gladness and garments of praise for the spirit of despair.[32] It was so before that awful Tuesday in September; it will always be so for us.

If we have truly received the life of Christ as our own, if we have been crucified with him, buried with him, and raised to new life in him, we cannot lay claim to any identity other than that of a servant.

If we have business cards to hand out, our logo should be the towel. Until Jesus returns, there will always be feet that need washing.

10

~

LIFE IN PROFOUND CONJUNCTION

THE DISCIPLINES OF FELLOWSHIP
AND CONFESSION

The Grace class started small.

Four of us, John and Margaret, Ken and I, gathered in a portable building cooled by a noisy window air conditioner and began praying about the people that God would bring to study with us. We agreed we were seeking a place of fellowship we hadn't found anywhere else—a place where authentic love could be expressed within a small group; a place rimmed with grace where people would feel safe to trust one another with intimate matters of the heart; a place that truly exemplified the biblical idea of fellowship.

The next week we were six, as another couple joined us, looking for a place where they could find prayer support and friendship as they dealt with the tragedy of a daughter's rape. In the coming weeks, singles joined us and shared their struggles, their triumphs, their dreams of ministry and service. An elderly couple, retired from Campus Crusade, came on board, sharing with us their wisdom and joy and enlisting our prayers for their granddaughter who suffers from cystic fibrosis. Ken and I found ourselves wrapped in love when we shared that our son's marriage was ending in divorce.

Over the years, some members have come and gone, but a strong core remains, and we have grown into a body that shares and cares. We have shared with one another the painful experiences of anorexia, financial loss, deaths of parents, broken engagements, and John's diagnosis of Lou Gehrig's disease. On any given Sunday, we may learn of a son or daughter's troubles with drugs, of new and increased problems with a special-needs child, of career crises, and of personal spiritual battles.

We have served together, and we have rejoiced together. We have celebrated engagements, marriages, births, new jobs, SAT scores, college scholarships, high-school football championships, and golf pars. We have shared in the commissioning of one of our own to vocational missionary service to Albania.

We are living proof of the truth of these words:

> Christian redemption is not devised to be a solitary thing, though each individual of course has a unique and direct relationship with God, and God alone is his or her Lord and Judge. But The Life is one that requires some regular and profound conjunction with others who share it. It is greatly diminished when that is lacking.[1]

In a small room on the second floor of a nondescript brick building, a group of disciples meets in "profound conjunction" with one another. A kind of incarnation occurs: God takes on human form. His people, indwelled by his Spirit, minister to one another in his name, listening, loving, serving, forgiving, and blessing one another with acceptance.

We have learned together that fellowship is one of the most valuable and joyous disciplines. And that confession is not only good for the soul, it is also good for the "Body."

Fellowship: A Means to Having God

"It is a manifestation of the humility of God that He creates a kingdom so rich in love that He should not be our all, but that others should be precious to us as well. Even in Eden, before the Fall, while Adam walked in Paradise with His God, even then God said, 'It is not good for man to be alone.'"[2]

This is an astounding truth—that God should have shaped us with hearts that seek one another, knowing that with others to love we might love him less. But he desired a creation made in his own image. Our need and desire for fellowship mirrors the mystery and glory of the incomprehensible nature of the Trinity, where the Father, the Son, and the Holy Spirit express and enjoy eternal, uninterrupted love.

This is the kind of fellowship that Jesus prayed for us to experience.

> I pray . . . that all of them may be one, Father, just as you are in me and I am in you. May they also be in us so that the world may believe you have sent me. I have given them the glory that you gave me, that they may be one as we are one: I in them and you in me. May they be brought to complete unity to let the world know that you sent me and have loved them even as you have loved me.
>
> . . . I have made you known to them, and will continue to

make you known in order that the love you have for me may
be in them and that I myself may be in them.[3]

In the expression of the discipline of fellowship we exhibit
the oneness that reigns joyously within the Trinity.

The Glory and Goal of Fellowship

Jesus said it clearly: his glory derives from his oneness with his
Father. He offers that same glory to us: oneness with the Father,
expressed in loving fellowship. This is one of the most mysterious
doctrines of the Christian faith. This is our glory—God is *in* us.
His presence draws us into fellowship with one another. Seeking
God, we seek his disciples; and seeking others of like faith, we
find God as well.

Teresa of Avila got it right when she said, "A good means to
having God is to speak with His friends."[4]

The goal of fellowship is twofold: it is to be a means of
exhibiting the greatest truth—that God came into the world
through his Son, Jesus; and it is to be a vivid and lively expression of love—God the Father's love for us, a love as passionate as
the love he has for his Son.

The Exercise of Fellowship

Fellowship is a discipline when, in the exercising of it, we oppose
selfishness and pride and an independent, exclusive spirit.
Fellowship occurs when we yank ourselves out of our lethargy or
out of our sloth and self-obsession and join with others in seeking
God, in expressing his love among ourselves, and in making him
known to others.

Dallas Willard wrote, "In fellowship we engage in common activities of worship, study, prayer, celebration and service with other disciples."[5]

A casual glance at the earthly life of Jesus shows his commitment to fellowship. He lived his entire adult life in community, and in communion, with others. This is an important fact for all of us who want to walk with God in obedience. We don't have the option of living in isolation. I am not allowed to label my spiritual life as "private," holding it to myself and sharing it only with God. Despite the romantic notion of the "lone wolf," there are no such animals in Christ's kingdom. We are all called to live in community and in communion. We are called to join our lives with others and to engage in the common activities of our faith.

In Jesus' life, fellowship often included shared meals. It included times of quiet prayer and discussion. The first model for small groups appeared when we saw Jesus pulling his disciples away from the crowd to be alone with him in a private place.

Fellowship, during Jesus' incarnation, included missionary trips and service projects (feeding thousands on a hillside). It included simple strolls through the Galilean countryside and excursions into local synagogues. It included weekends with friends, wedding celebrations, and visits to pools surrounded by the ill and infirm. It included fishing trips, shore breakfasts, and afternoon visits where children scampered about, offering living similes for teaching about kingdom life.

Jesus lived what he preached in the Sermon on the Mount: "Keep open house; be generous with your lives. By opening up to others, you'll prompt people to open up with God, this generous Father in heaven."[6]

Such a life poses certain risks, of course. Certainly, it was

risky for our Lord. He found himself in close contact with fishermen, tax collectors, lepers, and Pharisees. People pressed him for
miracles, pushed him into their problems, sought him out late at
night for private consultations. He was threatened, plotted
against, betrayed, and finally arrested and crucified. And because
the servant is not greater than the master, our lives as his disciples will not be risk-free.

Living in fellowship with others, we will often rub up against
people unlike ourselves. We will be pulled into problems that
will become our own; we'll be pressed for service we feel inadequate to give; and at times we'll feel as though our very lives are
being asked of us. But along with the struggles found in community come blessings and comforts and incalculable joys.

Through fellowship, we discover we are not alone in our
journey of faith. We find loving companions coming alongside us
as we travel, helping us over the difficult passages, lending us
support and encouragement when we encounter rough terrain.

In the first week after my son's marriage ended, a friend from
the Grace class invited me to lunch. Over salads and iced tea she
told me of her husband's first marriage more than thirty years
ago. It was a short and disastrous union, but God wrenched good
out of evil. The testimony of God's grace to a young man, of
healing and mercy, and finally the gift of this loving woman in
his life, made me smile with hope.

"It is a wonderful thing when a sick person finds another
wounded with that same sickness," wrote Teresa of Avila. "How
great the consolation to find you are not alone."[7]

This is one of the great joys of living in fellowship, in community. We discover others who understand us for having suffered our same maladies. We see how God worked in their lives,
and we gain hope and confidence that he will work for us too.

We see the surprising turn a life can take, in spite of disasters, difficulties, and unplanned heartaches, and we take courage.

Through fellowship we gain from the gifts of others and learn from them. We rely on the abilities of others to lead us, to stretch us, to teach us. And we share our joys and burdens with one another, benefiting from the unique insights and gifts that we share among ourselves.

No Place for Pride

Nothing is more opposed to the discipline of fellowship than the pursuit of personal power and prestige. Jesus made this point clear when the disciples argued among themselves about who would be the greatest in the kingdom.

In the unbelieving community, men and women use any excuse, any small shred of authority, to lord it over one another, Jesus told his quarreling friends. "Not so with you," he said. "Instead, whoever wants to become great among you must be your servant, and whoever wants to be first must be your slave—just as the Son of Man did not come to be served, but to serve, and to give his life as a ransom for many."[8]

Exercising the discipline of fellowship requires of us a clear understanding of the nature of service and the diligent exercise of humility and submission. It is essential for us to accept the truth that "if a person seeks human greatness, Christian community is not the place for [her]."[9]

Where Two or Three Are Gathered

Over the years I've known many Christians who claimed a popular television evangelist as their pastor. "I don't have to go to church or be a part of any group to worship God," one woman used to say. "I just tune in and have church here at home all by myself."

It is certainly simpler. There are no parking issues to deal with, no irritating people to relate to. She faces no pressure to "get involved."

It may be tempting at times to try to convince ourselves that we can seek God alone, that sitting in our homes, disconnected from others, we can have sufficient experience of God and grow in intimacy with him. But the prevailing evidence of the New Testament contradicts that notion. Believers comprise a "body," and every part is important to the effective, healthful functioning of that body.[10]

Certainly, there are times when we need to step back, withdraw for a few days to pray alone, and listen in quietness to God's Holy Spirit. Certainly, we should make time for retreats of solitude and silence. But we do not have the option of "dropping out" altogether. In fact, Jesus promised that we can expect to experience a kind of mysterious, transcendent sense of his presence when we get together with other Christians: "Where two or three come together in my name, there am I with them."[11]

We can grasp his meaning only if we look again at his prayer in John 17. In the hours before Jesus' death, the passion of his heart for his disciples and the disciples yet to be born was that they live in fellowship that mirrored the fellowship of the Father and the Son. That they would be one, as the Father and Son are one—that they would love one another and share in the life of God in each other, each partaking in the glory of God.

We must not miss this vital truth: God's deepest desire for us is that we comprehend and live in the reality of the joy of the triune God. That we share in that unity, that we revel in that oneness.

But it is as George MacDonald wrote, "There can be no oneness where there is only one. For the very beginnings of unity there must be two."[12]

The Discipline of Confession

We cannot live an authentic life, in fellowship with God or his creatures, without the discipline of confession. For the discipline of confession is always the acknowledgment of truth. It is the recognition of reality—in our lives, in the lives of others, in the universe. It is the acceptance of our condition before God and our relationship to others. It is agreement with truth.

Confession offers us the possibility of oneness, the hope of deep fellowship—with God and with his people.

When we confess our sin to God, we oppose pride and an attitude of spiritual independence. We embrace the truth about our position before God.

In its first utterance, confession may be a whimper or a howl as we initially grasp the truth of our frailty and depravity and sink against the heart of God. There we accept this knowledge: without the Father's love, we will die. Without his provision for life, for salvation, we will perish.

This is our first confession, and heaven rejoices.

We fix our eyes on the Son, who gave his life to give us ours. We begin to learn the meaning of holiness. We learn to love his face, the sound of his voice.

Confession then becomes a daily exercise. We may still whimper or howl. We may whisper or scream, angry at our constant wandering, burdened by the guilt of our sinning. Time after time we lie back against the Father's heart and accept again his love and tenderness, his forgiveness made available to us at the cross.

We learn to live with the truth that as long as we live in the presence of sin, sin will be present in us. Even the most saintly among us cannot escape this reality. It was Paul the Apostle who moaned, "For what I do is not the good I want to do; no, the evil I do not want to do—this I keep on doing."[13]

But we learn too that confession leads to peace and rest. This promise is our strong consolation: "If we confess our sins, He is faithful and righteous to forgive us our sins and to cleanse us from all unrighteousness."[14]

If we as sinful creatures are ever to experience fellowship, oneness, with our holy Creator, confession must occur.

If we are to maintain that fellowship and oneness of spirit between a Father and his children, confession must be a daily discipline. For where there is no confession of sin, there can be no forgiveness. There can be no unity and no authentic life.

Confessing Our Vulnerabilities

"I need you all to pray for me," Pam told the Grace class one Sunday morning. "I've just found out that the daughter I gave up for adoption thirty-nine years ago wants to meet me."

There were no gasps, no whispers. John, up at the podium, grinned and said, "Wow! That's fantastic! You must have all kinds of feelings. How do you want us to pray?"

Even as I write this I remember the awe that surged through me that day as I looked around at this "ragamuffin" class—a group of misfits, mostly, that hadn't quite found a home anyplace else in our large church. A woman sitting next to Pam reached out and squeezed her hand. Another, behind her, stretched forward to pat her back. One by one, we sniffled and wiped at our eyes. John grabbed a box of Kleenex from a shelf up front, snatched a tissue for himself, and then handed the box to the front row.

On some Sundays, Dick fills in at the podium. His vulnerability stuns me. Many weeks he shares the struggles involved in making a blended family work. We are a fellowship made strong and lively by the discipline of confession.

Believers, knowing themselves to be safe in the love of God and among his people, dare to expose their vulnerabilities, their sins. They reveal their true selves, choosing to live authentically in a world that seems often to prefer disguise. They know the risks. But they choose to be real.

They choose to live in the truth of who they are, what they have done, and what they are going through on the way to Glory. They choose to enter into the experience of oneness, of fellowship, through the discipline of confession.

They choose to welcome, to listen without censure, without finger-pointing, to the confessions of others. And then to minister faithfully in prayer on their behalf.

At no time in our lives will we be more like Jesus than in those moments when we are listening, loving, and interceding for others before the throne of grace. Charged with the work of a royal priesthood, we have the privilege of emulating him who is our High Priest, who is at this very moment listening to our hearts, seeing our needs, and bringing them before his Father's throne, asking his Father to do for us what he is doing for the Son.

And what is the Father doing for the Son? He is loving him, sharing his glory with him, sharing his joy with him, disclosing his will to him, ever and always celebrating the love of a Father and a Son.

Confessing Our Sins to One Another

James didn't mince words. He said it clearly: "Confess your sins to each other."[15]

Wisdom, and the context of the Scripture, would add: make sure you do your confessing to a mature, loving believer who understands and practices the other spiritual disciplines, most especially humility, secrecy, and prayer.

In the company of such a believer, your confession is safe, and the good it will do you is immeasurable.

I speak from experience. I have two special friends, in addition to Ken, with whom I often confess my sins. With Ken, it is usually a spontaneous confession, not a planned event. We talk about it, sometimes we cry about it together, and then he prays for me. With Carolyn, confession erupts over lunch, over coffee, and she assures me of her love for me and promises to pray. Sometimes she tells me she struggles with my same sin, and I am relieved to know I'm not alone.

With Margaret, I plan my confession. I make note of the weaknesses and failings, the deliberate and willful sins for which I want her to keep me accountable. I write them down, take them with me to our prayer time, and then I tell her where I have failed. She listens, she loves me. Sometimes my sin is hers as well; often I am her confessor.

In the presence of each of these to whom I confess my sins I experience the reality of Christ. I see them listen and love me, regardless of my wickedness. They cannot absolve me of my sin, but royal priests that they are,[16] they "handle" the sacrifice, always pointing me to the Lamb of God, whose blood cleanses me and relieves me of the burden of guilt.

Dietrich Bonhoeffer wrote, "A man who confesses his sins in the presence of a brother knows that he is no longer alone with

himself; he experiences God in the reality of the other person."[17]
It is true for women as well.

Walter Wangerin Jr. said:

> I suggest that you involve other Christians who will keep your
> confidence absolute, who believe in forgiveness, and who love
> the Lord Jesus. Confess to the Lord in their hearing. Allow
> them gently to question you until you have truly disclosed the
> whole of your sinning. And when all has been confessed out
> loud, then hear in the mouths of your friends the clear and cer-
> tain assurance of Jesus' forgiveness. [18]

Jesus' Exercise of Confession

Jesus asked nothing of us that he did not ask of himself. He too
exercised the discipline of confession. His was not the confession of
sin—he was holy, perfectly righteous in every aspect of his being—
but he lived the whole of his life as a vibrant expression of truth.

Jesus' life expressed the truth about the nature of God, his
character; about the human condition, its eternal destiny; about
his longing for his bride; about his love for his Father. It was
through the exercise of confession that he revealed himself to us
and made known to us the heart of God.

Not stoic or reserved, not standoffish, Jesus entered fully into
the human experience. He did not hold back his tears at the
death of his friend, Lazarus. In the Garden when he brought his
friends with him to pray, he confessed his vulnerability. He said
to them, "My soul is overwhelmed with sorrow to the point of
death. Stay here and keep watch with me."[19] And when he found
them sleeping, he did not hide his heartbreak: "Could you men
not keep watch with me for one hour?"[20]

To look at Jesus is to see an authentic life, a transparent life.

He concealed nothing about his nature, nothing about his heart. And in revealing himself, he revealed the Father. "I and the Father are one," he said.[21]

And the Jews picked up stones to kill him.

A life of authenticity and transparency is not a life of safety. Revealing our true selves means we will risk being misunderstood, disliked, and rejected, as Jesus was. At times, even among the fellowship of other believers, we will find living a transparent life to be painful, because Christians are not always loving, understanding, or accepting. It was true for Jesus—his betrayer was one of his disciples. It may be true for us as well.

But what are our alternatives? If we refuse to live as Jesus lived—honestly, openly, authentically—we have only one option: a life of facades and superficial relationships.

Not Forgetting Secrecy

All of us have known women who live so openly, so honestly, that every conversation with them is a gushing river of information that threatens to flood us with its force. We wish they would dam things up a bit. "Liz" was such a woman. You could stand in the aisles at church and see people walk out of their way to avoid the torrent that they knew awaited them if they engaged Liz in conversation.

We've all been in the company of people who tell us more than they should, more than we want to know—maybe we are some of them. It's important to know that this isn't necessarily the exercise of the discipline of confession. Although confession does call us to honesty and authenticity, it does not preclude the exercise of silence or secrecy. It does not preclude discernment about when and to whom and how much of ourselves to disclose.

I find it fascinating that in some instances, Jesus told people he healed to keep quiet about what he had done.[22] Always aware of his Father's plan, his Father's timing, Jesus never acted out of urgency, anxiety, or a need for attention and applause. He always acted out of love for his Father and love for his Father's will.

In our desire to exercise the discipline of confession, to live truthfully, Jesus' example is important. He recognized that there were moments when full disclosure was not appropriate. On some occasions the most holy, obedient thing to do was to keep silent, or to advise others to keep silent.

Confession, exercised under the direction of the Holy Spirit, will always result in honesty and transparency. But it will not always require a verbal recitation detailing every intricate spiritual experience.

Confession always offers us the opportunity to live in the reality of who we are in Christ—daughters of the King of kings. But it will also call us to recognize that as his children, we are to seek unity with his plans and desires for us. We are to seek the unity of the whole body of believers. In certain situations, that may require us to confide quietly in God alone, instead of confessing aloud in the presence of others.

Henri Nouwen wrote: "Do not tell everyone your story. . . . God will send to you the people with whom you can share your anguish, who can lead you closer to the true source of love."[23]

Sustained by Each Other

Living honestly in fellowship with other human beings begins with a decision to live honestly before God, choosing to be engaged in fellowship with him, learning from him, listening to him with intent to obey.

Exercising the disciplines of fellowship and confession will take us into relationships and situations that will challenge our faith and test our love for God and his people. It is good to remember that God gave us these disciplines to aid us in our growth toward Christlikeness. They, like the other spiritual disciplines, are God's means of helping us get to know him as he really is; they are his means of training us to recognize and experience his love and grace; they are aids for training us to live free of artifice and bondage to appearances.

I love Dallas Willard's thought: "The fire of God kindles higher as the brands are heaped together and each is warmed by the other's flame. The members of the body must be in contact if they are to sustain and be sustained by each other."[24]

Such contact often may be painful. It means we will at times have to confront sin, address wrong behaviors, and acknowledge our weaknesses, our besetting sins. Unless we are experiencing the Holy Spirit's daily leading and asking him to cultivate his fruit in our lives, fellowship can be damaged. Instead of communion, chaos. Instead of confession, gossip.

This is the great risk of living openly in close fellowship with other human beings. It will either sustain us or destroy us. Unless we are exercising the disciplines of humility, submission, secrecy, and prayer, along with fellowship and confession, the body's very integral work of pointing others to the love of God may degenerate into the futile, ferocious work of finger-pointing.

Theology of a Kiss

In the Navajo culture, "finger-pointing," in the literal sense, is considered an act of violence. "The hands are deceptive things without brains and are hired things without souls," a Navajo once explained to a *biligaana*.[25] So a Navajo never points a finger—not at a person or at an inanimate object, not even to indicate a road or a direction. To gesture, the *Dinéh* use the body, the head, but most often the lips, with a gentle pursing, much like a kiss.

There is deep theology for us in these Navajo ways.

In order to live in fellowship with one another, exercising confession, loving each other, and expressing the unity of the Father and the Son, we will need to give up the habit of finger-pointing. We will need to fall on the strength of God to deter us when we are tempted to judge harshly.

We will need to abandon all weapons of violence against one other—gossip, lies, impatience, and unrealistic expectations.

We will need to learn to move toward one another with tenderness; to gesture, figuratively, with a kiss.

*   *   *

The intimacy and fellowship of the Grace class was not an instant phenomenon. It has grown, sometimes slowly, although steadily, over the years. As a group, we stay connected between Sundays through e-mail, phone calls, acts of service and prayer. When a newcomer joins us, there is no immediate expectation of confession or disclosure, but often it occurs soon. The atmosphere of honesty and vulnerability is hard to resist.

Richard Foster wrote:

If we know that the people of God are first a fellowship of sinners, we are freed to hear the unconditional call of God's love and to confess our needs openly before our brothers and sisters. . . . We know we are not alone in our sin. In acts of mutual confession we release the power that heals.[26]

This is the heart of fellowship and confession—the experience and expression of eternal oneness; the exhibit and expression of the eternal, unchanging truth: God is love.

By this we are sustained.

11
~

THE DELIGHT OF HEAVEN

THE DISCIPLINES OF WORSHIP
AND CELEBRATION

*L*ate one night the Navajo game warden phoned my father and asked, "You want to shoot a bear, Larry? Get your rifle and I'll pick you up in fifteen minutes."

For weeks, a large black bear had been destroying cornfields and vegetable gardens and terrorizing sheep herds. The warden had made several attempts to stop the rampage, or at least move it off the reservation, but nothing had worked.

"The bear has to be killed," the warden told my dad as they crept through a cornfield in the middle of the night, armed with a flashlight and a thirty-ought-six. The warden held the light, my father the gun.

In the ancient Navajo way, a bear is usually worshiped. Even this Navajo, a recent convert to Christianity, couldn't quite rid himself of the idea that he should revere this big, black, shaggy creature. He couldn't shake the fear that he might jeopardize his spiritual safety if he killed it. He would let the Anglo take the risk.

Such worship is not unique to the Navajo. In any culture, on any continent it is common to find creatures worshiping creatures. Here in my Texas hometown, all around me I see men and women worshiping each other, their children, their families, their pets.

The human heart craves something to worship, and left to itself, it will worship almost anything. Anything, that is, that will camouflage its own deficiencies and give it a sense of significance, of value—even if that significance is an illusion, even if that value is false. We worship our money, success, goals, leisure activities, our stuff. And any thought of slaying one of these "gods" terrifies us, because we too have linked them with our safety.

We will worship. We have to worship. At times, we aren't sure precisely what it is we're worshiping. We don't always know whom we should worship.

Even the most devout, the most godly, can worship in error. The apostle John, on two occasions, told of being overwhelmed by the shimmering beauty and awesome strength of an angel. He was ready to drop to his knees in worship, but the angel stopped him.[1]

Confusion about worship occurs everywhere, in everyone. It was this confusion Jesus addressed when he told the Samaritan woman, "You don't know what you worship." Dorothy Sayers added, Jesus was "apparently under the impression that it might be desirable, on the whole, to know what one was worshipping."[2]

Preventing John before he could kneel in error, the angel said, "Worship God."

In scores of passages in the Psalms, we read, "Worship the Lord." "Worship at his footstool," the psalmist wrote.[3] The New Testament has many instructions to worship God as well as examples of genuine worship. If we seriously yearn for intimacy with God, we must learn to worship him, and only him, in spirit and in truth.[4]

When true spiritual worship becomes a consistent, daily habit for us, the exercise of the discipline of celebration won't be far behind.

Spiritual activities that elevate God in our hearts, worship and celebration train us to give God what is due him: our adoration, our praise. They are the vivid and lively expressions of absolute trust in his extravagant goodness, his power, his sovereign wisdom and love.

Through worship and celebration we engage in the joy of heaven.

Worship: Living in Response to God

"In worship God gathers His people to himself as center: 'The Lord reigns.' Worship is a meeting at the center so that our lives are centered in God and not lived eccentrically. We worship so that we live in response to and from this center, the Living God."[5]

God is, in fact, the center of all things: "Through him all things were made,"[6] and "in him we live and move and have our being."[7]

Worshiping God means responding with praise and adoration to the truth of all that he is, all that he has done, all that he is doing, and all that he will do.

We live in appropriate response to the fact that he is the Creator, we are the creatures. We live in the reality of that truth, recognizing the surpassing worth of the God who made us, who loves us tenderly, and who sustains us by his power and grace.

Knowing Enough to Worship

The Psalms offer us the best expressions of worship we will ever hear this side of heaven. Many conceived in the irony of suffering they teach us that neither circumstances nor scenery can be the basis for our worship.

David spent his adolescence in the fields with sheep. During his early manhood, he led a band of guerilla fighters, living in caves, hiding out in desert badlands, dodging death at the hands of the man who was once his friend. As an adult, David experienced a life scarred by family crises, rape and murder, wars, and occasions of blatant, cruel sin. Yet the predominant image of this warrior-king is this: he lived in humble response to the unfathomable greatness of God.

George MacDonald asked the question: "O Lord, dare we imagine Thee as good as we hope Thou art?"[8] David answered with a resounding "Yes!"

> Sing to God, sing praise to his name,
> extol him who rides on the clouds—
> his name is the LORD—and rejoice before him—[9]

> Blessed are those you choose and bring near to live in your
> Courts! We are filled with the good things of your house,
> of your holy temple.[10]

> Come and see what God has done,
> how awesome his works in man's behalf.[11]

Out of David's mouth came these breathless musings on the greatness of God. How did he become so intimately acquainted with this truth?

He told us: "I have seen you in the sanctuary and beheld your power and your glory." "You answer us with awesome deeds."[12] He learned to know God, by faith. And he saw God act on his behalf. His testimony: "I have seen what God is like, and I know what God can do."

From this, worship sprang into life.

The Spiritual Act of Worship

We walk into a pretty church, take a seat, and feel something swell in our chests as music soars.

We stand on a cliff and stare off at a majestic mountain range and feel our hearts pump a little faster, a little stronger, as the beauty fills us, overwhelms us.

Is this worship? It might be.

But if you live in Texas, how often are you going to get to stand on a mountain peak? Do you have to wait for the choir anthem on a Sunday morning in order to worship?

Is once or twice a week enough? How often should the Christian worship God? What constitutes worship? When does it become a discipline?

Paul answered these questions for us in his letter to the Roman church. We perform the spiritual act of worship, he wrote, when we present our bodies as a living sacrifice, holy and pleasing to God.[13]

Of all the passages that discuss worship, to me this is the most definitive; however, it both clarifies and complicates the matter for me. On the one hand, I see that I can worship anywhere, any time. The Spirit of God lives in me. My body is his temple. At any moment I can climb up on the "altar" and present myself as a living sacrifice. I can worship Monday through Saturday, as well as on Sunday; I can worship when I'm perusing

the shelves of the corner grocery store, when I'm shuffling mail at
my desk, or when I'm jogging through neighborhood streets as
easily as I can in a cathedral or on a mountaintop.

But when Paul introduced "sacrifice" into the discussion, I
have to revisit those occasions when I enjoyed warm, fuzzy feelings and called it worship. When beauty surrounded me and all
was right with my world, did the feelings of those moments constitute true worship?

We've all had those occasions of sweet emotion, when on
some level we were aware of our relationship to God—the creature to the Creator—and felt awe at all that is good and beautiful
in our lives. Spontaneous adoration of God erupted. Worship
occurred. God was central to our thoughts. All other concerns
faded. God was our focus.

Whether we realized it or not, a kind of sacrifice was occurring. Overshadowed by the awesomeness of God, our own egos
let God have first place. And worship happened.

But worship, in those instances, was not necessarily a discipline. Nothing inside us warred with God for center stage.
Inspired by beauty, art, music, or a noble theme, our hearts
bowed gladly, without resistance. It is only later, when inspira-
tion has fled and the mystical sense of the presence of God has
dissipated, that worship becomes a discipline.

When we've had to leave the majestic mountain's view;
when we've returned to our homes in the suburbs to deal with
the reality of our lives—broken lawn mowers, low SAT scores,
employee downsizing, terrorist threats, a crashing economy, and
the danger of anthrax spores—this is when we learn the value of
the discipline of worship. When ugliness, not beauty, fills our
view, worship becomes a discipline.

When, against all our feelings to the contrary, all our fears, we choose to believe in the sovereign goodness of God and make him the focal point of our lives, we are exercising the discipline of worship. We sacrifice the tendency of our nature to bemoan his dealings with us; we battle ego in those moments when the self wants to be enthroned, and we climb up on the altar, becoming a living sacrifice, slaying our will, embracing God's.

When we have sacrificed our human reasoning and exchanged our desires for God's, we have exercised the discipline of worship. When we have praised him even though every molecule in us is crying out against our circumstances; when we have deliberately directed our focus to him and his promises of faithfulness, in spite of losses large and small, we have exercised the discipline of worship.

We do it at times falteringly, even fearfully; but we do it because we believe that he is worthy of our total trust, and because we have learned that, without the discipline of worship, all possibility of intimacy with God will elude us.

How to Worship

So, then, what does worship look like? If I truly desire to worship God, what kind of activities should I engage in?

Dallas Willard wrote:

> In worship we engage ourselves with, dwell upon, and express the greatness, beauty, and goodness of God through thought and the use of words, rituals and symbols. We do this alone as well as in union with God's people. To worship is to see God as worthy, to ascribe great worth to Him.[14]

The integration of other disciplines, as well as sacrifice, gives worship its shape and expression. Through meditation, we ponder the greatness of God and respond with worship. Through study, we discover the overwhelming grandeur of God, and we can't help but bow in worship.

In prayer we offer our words of worship to the Father.

In solitude, we sacrifice social interaction and bow before him without distraction, without interruption.

In silence, we choose to be quiet in his presence, to listen to his voice, acknowledging that he is there, he is available, and he is involved in our affairs. We worship by sacrificing our own words, our own opinions, and bow to his judgments, his thoughts.

In fellowship, we join with others in recognizing the wonders of God, in singing praise to him, in reading Psalms together, and in listening to the teaching of truth. In confession, we tell each other of his wonderful dealings with us, extolling the greatness of God, spurring one another on to greater heights of worship.

When we serve, we engage in activities that reveal his character and we place him at the heart of our endeavors, making him central, not ourselves. We point to his greatness, not our own, directing all applause toward heaven.

In the exercise of every discipline undertaken in faith and with humility, we worship God, for we are placing him at the center of our lives. We are forgoing other pursuits, other attractions, for the sake of knowing him better, experiencing him intimately.

This is the goal. How difficult it is to accomplish.

Cultivating Worship

Our human cravings for greatness, for control, for power, play havoc with the tender call of the Spirit that urges us to "worship in spirit and in truth."

How do we quiet those cravings? How do we worship when

our egos are begging to be enthroned in the place of honor that belongs to God alone?

How do we cultivate a life of worship?

My daughter, Molly, once gave me a vivid picture of what needs to happen for us to be able to drop to our knees before God in willing, loving worship.

Several years ago, we were visiting Rome, just the two of us, on a mother-daughter tour of the great capitals of Europe. We had visited magnificent cathedrals, seeing architecture and beauty that, by comparison, make most American churches look like potting sheds. Our last stop after a long day of sightseeing was the Sistine Chapel.

I watched Molly walk in and look up. Her eyes widened, her jaw dropped, and she settled down on a bench where she just sat and stared upward in silence. I know I should have done the same thing, but I was more charmed by watching my daughter, who only moments earlier had been bored, tired, and wondering how much longer the tour would last. Now, here, in the presence of this transcendent beauty, all her thoughts about hunger and weariness fled. Her face upturned, her eyes focused on the startling beauty of Michelangelo's art. In the presence of such masterful greatness, nothing else mattered. Nothing distracted her, not even the noise of milling tourists shushed by chapel guards.

I love the memory of that day. When I think of worship, I see the rapturous expression on Molly's face. She embodied worship, for it is a *looking up*. It is gazing at God, at the Son, Christ Jesus, letting everything else fade into nothingness and seeing only his splendor and grace.

This is the one essential imperative of our faith, this looking up. The transforming work of God occurs within us in that first moment when the crucified Jesus fills our vision, when we see him hanging there, the innocent for the guilty, and we drop to our knees in repentance. Until the moment we see his face in glory, we continue to look up. We "fix our eyes on Jesus, the author and perfecter of our faith."[15]

I didn't always understand this. There was a time not so long ago when my spiritual temperature was tepid, at best. My desire for God small, selfish. My son was away at college and my daughter was getting ready to go. I was preparing for an empty nest even as Ken's travel schedule increased. My work was tedious; life seemed inglorious, worship sporadic, if occurring at all. I was going through the motions of faith without any enthusiasm or pleasure. Then, at the gentle prompting of the Holy Spirit, I began reading the Gospels.

Beginning in Matthew, I slowly, steadily worked my way through the story of Jesus. Revisiting the manger in Bethlehem, I felt as though I was seeing the mystery and majesty of the Nativity for the first time. God, becoming a baby, brought his glory near without terrifying us, without consuming us with the heat and fire of it—the same glory that would have burned Moses to ash if God hadn't hidden him behind tons of granite.

There, sheltered in the crease of a rock, God covered Moses with his hand and let Moses look at his retreating presence. The light and glory of it irradiated Moses' face so brightly he had to cover it with a veil.

How different the scene in Bethlehem. God visited his creation, but instead of hiding them from the heat of his glory, he hid himself, shrouding his glory in swaddling clothes; inviting us to draw near without fear. His omnipotent splendor could live among us wrapped in humanity and we would not shrivel in terror.

We could watch him grow into manhood, displaying all the

attributes of his heavenly Father. We could eat with him, travel with him, converse with him, touch him, and begin to know him. The weakness and vulnerability of his humanity would free us to love him or hate him; worship him or murder him.

For days, I lingered at the manger, letting the profound implications of the Incarnation wash over me before I moved on to walk the hills of Galilee with the young Carpenter-turned-Rabbi.

I tagged along with the motley band he called friends and thought, *I'd have fit right in with these guys.* Often doubting and scared, they too were sometimes confused, ill suited to discipleship. Like a bratty little sister, I probably would have bickered with James and John, fighting for the seat closest to Jesus in the kingdom.

In every verse, every chapter, I saw the living God in human garb exhibiting patience with the slow-witted, kindness to the poor and sick. A spellbinding storyteller, he mesmerized huge audiences, holding them long past the dinner hour, and then feeding them before sending them home.

Jesus calming the sea, raising the dead, casting out demons; Jesus clearing the temple, eating with reprobates, and finally dying like a common criminal so all charges against me could be dropped—I couldn't escape the picture that emerged: this God who loves me is beautiful. Weak in his humanity and willing to die, yet stronger than death, he is mightier than the evil that crucified him.

Today, two thousand years later, he welcomes my friendship. He invites my company. Against all human reason, he pursues a relationship with me. After reading the final words in the last Gospel, I had to bow in awe and echo the psalmist's words, "My King and my God"![16]

I've learned this truth: when worship is difficult, when my spirit resists, the only thing that will unlock my stubborn knees and pull me into reverence is a fresh view of Jesus. Although thousands of years have passed since David's discovery, the truth of it still resonates: when we have seen what God can do, and we know what God is like, worship is our only reasonable response.

Celebration: Living with a Light Heart

In worship, we place God at the very center of our conscious being. We respond to his magnificent greatness by setting aside our own self-interest and selfish pursuits to make him our focus, his purposes our priority. In celebration, we respond to his sovereign goodness with a light heart and a joyful spirit.

Sometimes celebration just happens. The goodness of God is so tangible, so obvious, we feel as though our hearts are textured with his triumphs. Our every thought is tinged with light; our souls become party places.

Such occasions of delight are delicious, but they are just that: occasional. Packed in between the special moments of spontaneous spiritual celebration are many hours, many days and years of ordinary living. The discipline of celebration, however, invites us to keep the party hats handy. It invites us to recognize that, as children of the living God, we are never without reason for joy and celebration. It invites us to live amid the drab and the mundane with a playful spirit, knowing a good and sovereign God is watching over us. His tender gaze never wanders. His kind intentions toward us never waver.

It invites us to experience transcendent joy *in the midst of* the bland and the ordinary; *in spite of* evil, ugliness, and terror.

Cause for Celebration

The human tendency to despair is natural. All around us are very real reasons for fear and unease.

Even before the terrorists' attacks of September 11, 2001, we could find ample cause for worry and negativism. Since then, as we have waged "America's new war," we have wondered if we will ever feel good again, if the weight of grief and anxiety will ever lift. We have struggled, as individuals and as a nation, to determine what is appropriate as we live with this new reality and the insidious threat of evil that haunts our homeland.

For a while it seemed as though laughter was dead. Celebration was inappropriate—like playing jump rope at a funeral. But in spite of the terror and sadness that stalked us, a gentle celebration pulsed quietly. Like a beating heart that refuses to quit, even though the rest of the body is mangled and bloody, the discipline of celebration kept hope alive within the body of Christ.

We are "sorrowful, yet always rejoicing," wrote the apostle Paul, describing perfectly the discipline of celebration.[17]

It is a celebration that transcends events and individuals, catastrophes and personal tragedies.

It is a mind-set that accepts the horrors of our reality and responds with the appropriate demeanor, while at the same time embracing the invisible, eternal, joy-filled realities: God is love, he is sovereign, he is present, and he continues to express his goodness in extravagant, exuberant acts of grace.

Taking the Long View

Peter told us to celebrate our inheritance. When everything else looks dismal, he said, remember all that you have in Christ Jesus.

He acknowledged the very real difficulties of the human existence: "Though now for a little while you may have to suffer grief in all kinds of trials." And then he added, "Rejoice in this: the magnificent inheritance that awaits you."[18]

We can celebrate even when we are suffering, because we have an inheritance that a terrorist attack can't destroy. A plunging Dow Jones can't diminish it. Disease or dysfunction can't wipe it out. Our new birth is accomplished—we are daughters of the King of kings—and our heritage is secure.

These things are so magnificent, so astounding, and this grace so amazing that the angels yearn to look into it.[19] They would love to study it, figure it out, discuss it with God, but God holds the majesty of it close to his heart to be unwrapped for his children only, in their presence, when finally they rush into his arms. The angels, boggled, can only speculate at what the Father withholds from them and shake their heads in wonder.

When the events of life are so awful, so sad, that we aren't sure we have permission to laugh, the discipline of celebration says, "Remember this: your Father is holding treasures for you—treasures you can't even begin to imagine! Don't allow the visible terrors and traumas of the day to rob you of the joy of the invisible treasures that God holds in trust for your eternal pleasure."

Don't exchange your hope for despair.

With the words of the great preacher E. V. Hill, God reminds us, "This ain't it, folks!" Once we arrive in heaven, we will realize that the grief and struggle and painful experiences of this life were nothing compared to the majestic wonders of heaven. Oswald Chambers learned this while he lived, and it made all the difference as he served God in Africa. "Learn to take the long view," he wrote, "and you will breathe the benediction of God among the squalid things that surround you."[20]

I keep these words of John Piper on an index card on my desk so I never forget this truth:

> God's omnipotent exuberance to do us good is one of the most freeing discoveries a human can make. O that we might believe it and savor it and bring it to mind again and again until it is our very nature to feel the truth that the "godly are destined for unknown and inconceivable happiness."[21]

Do we know this? Do we believe it in the very deepest places in our soul? Do we savor it and bring it to mind often?

The discipline of celebration calls us to remember and be convinced that, for God's beloved, the best is yet to come.

No Excuses Accepted

We all know people who find it hard to celebrate, even when life is great and all is well with their world. Maybe you are one of them. Depending on your temperament, you may find it easier to exercise the disciplines of study, or prayer, or service, than to engage in celebration. You may find it more natural to moan and lament than to celebrate. But our temperament does not give us an out.

Temperament doesn't exempt us from any of the spiritual disciplines. We don't receive an excused absence from service because we are phlegmatic—more spectator than participant. God doesn't exempt us from solitude and silence because we are sanguine and expressive by nature; nor does he excuse us from fellowship because we are not "people persons." In the same way, he does not lower his expectations that we live with a light heart just because a personality test labeled us melancholic.

As the beloved children of God, clasped in the tenderness of our Father, all of us, regardless of our personality type, have good reason to celebrate. But how many of us really live each day with a light heart?

If gladness doesn't describe us, if celebration is a rare occurrence, maybe we have fixated on what feels easy and natural to our nature—pessimism or negativism—instead of focusing on what the nature of Christ in us is able to accomplish.

Maybe it is a temperament issue. For many of us, it could be. But then again, maybe it's tedium. Maybe we've become bored with the tale. If so, Dorothy Sayers would have little patience with us. She wrote of the

> outline of the official story—the tale of the time when God was the underdog and got beaten, when He submitted to the conditions He had laid down and became a man like the men He had made, and the men He had made broke Him and killed Him. This is the dogma we find so dull—this terrifying drama of which God is the victim and the hero. If this is dull, then what, in Heaven's name, is worthy to be called exciting?[22]

And what, in heaven's name, is worthy of celebration?

Jesus was "emphatically not a dull man in His human lifetime, and if He was God, there can be nothing dull about God either."[23]

If celebration is infrequent or, at best, a halfhearted chore, maybe we have lost the sense of the mystery and majesty of the story of God.

The psalmist wrote:

> But let *all* who take refuge in you be glad;
> let them *ever* sing for joy.[24]

May the righteous be glad
and rejoice before God;
may they be happy and joyful.[25]

God calls all believers to exuberant faith that overflows into celebration. Temperament doesn't exempt us. Tedium doesn't excuse us.

Strength: A By-Product of Celebration

It is an unarguable fact: strength and celebration are intricately connected in theology.

Show me a woman who is joyful, who exercises the discipline of celebration, and I will show you a strong woman, unbowed and unbroken by life's difficulties. "The joy of the Lord is your strength," wrote Nehemiah.[26]

Here's the context: Nehemiah had led the nation of Israel in the rebuilding of Jerusalem's torched gates and broken walls. The work finally completed, the people gathered inside the city walls to listen as Ezra the priest read to them from the law of God. Their hearts broke; repentance brought them to their knees. Worship erupted, and they couldn't stop weeping.

Finally, Nehemiah shouted, "Enough! No more grieving! Go celebrate this sacred event! Enjoy good food and share with your neighbors who don't have anything prepared. Your strength will be derived from the joy you find in God."

Sorrow had dulled their hearing. He shouted again, "Be still! Do not grieve."

Gradually, the crowd broke up. Small groups gathered to eat and "celebrate with great joy, because they now understood the words that had been made known to them."[27]

We can't miss this: the people were able to celebrate because they embraced the revealed truth of God—that they were loved and forgiven. Celebration gave birth to strength.

For the woman of God, the implications are great. If we want to be strong women of faith, we have to grasp the truth of our belovedness—believe it, enter into it fully. We must learn to live in the reality of our position in Christ, truly know that we are forgiven, cherished, adored by God. When we can do this, celebration, like the joy of a bride, will erupt within us and give birth to unimaginable strength.

Holding On to Wonder

George MacDonald wrote, "To cease to wonder is to fall from the childlike to the commonplace—most undivine of all intellectual moods. Our nature can never be at home among things that are not wonderful to us."[28] Through the exercise of the discipline of celebration, we are able to be "at home" among the things that are wonderful.

With the celebration of every Christmas, we enter, childlike, into the wonder of the Incarnation.

With the celebration of every baptism, we enter again into the sacred mystery of Christ's death, his burial and resurrection.

With the celebration of the Lord's Supper, as we share his Passion, we partake of the nature of God the Son, who in childlike trust abandoned himself to the will of the Father. Mystery and wonder engulf us.

With the celebration of every holiday—every holy day, every marriage, every birth, and yes, every believer's death, we write in our flesh the story of God with us—the romantic Lover, the heroic King, the prodigal's Father, the triumphant Warrior.

Through celebration, we become living metaphors of the kingdom of God, where joy and gladness are never ending, never quenched.

And on the ordinary days, the in-between days, in every activity that expresses the reality of God *among* us, the reality of God *in* us, and the reality of God *for* us, we step into mystery with childlike faith. And we experience the wonder of God.

With every year I live, I become more convinced that without the discipline of celebration, we distance ourselves from mystery, from transcendence. We make ourselves aliens among the things of God, strangers in a place that should be home.

Wanted: Women of Celebration

We all know the long list King Lemuel's mother gave him, itemizing what he should look for in a wife. We've tortured ourselves with that list, ridiculed it, and tried to adapt it to our twenty-first-century reality. When I read that a wise woman brings her food from afar, for me that means she's learned the best places to call for take-out.

But one passage in that chapter needs no cultural revisions. It is as poignant and appropriate for me today, in Texas, as it was when the Proverbs writer recorded it in Jerusalem a few thousand years ago. "Find yourself a woman who can laugh at the days to come," he wrote. "Find a woman with a light heart."[29]

Those words never have been more timely, or more relevant.

Since God posted angel-guards at Eden's gate, this world has been a scary place. Every generation has fought its own wars, grieved over its own losses, and faced an uncertain future. Today, the present is filled with threats and hazards too awful to contemplate. The future offers possibilities of horrors almost unimaginable. Against this backdrop, a lighthearted woman is truly a prize. Her value is far above rubies. Who can find one?

Most of the women I know aren't terribly overwhelmed by Proverbs' description of a virtuous woman. Most of us can put food on our tables, even if it's macaroni and cheese from a box; we can figure out ways to dress our kids on a tight budget; we can handle our finances, balance a checkbook, and invest on-line. We can perform our jobs, volunteer in our communities, behave respectably when necessary, and find ways to make our families proud of us. Some of us can sew, some can garden, some can change the oil in the family car. But how many of us can do these things with a smile?

How many of us are full of laughter and hope? How many of us light our homes with celebration and fun and bathe our families with sweetness?

This challenge is not for wives and mothers only, but for all women. All of us have the privilege of reflecting the nature of Christ, who was anointed with the oil of gladness.[30] All of us have the privilege of bringing joy into our environments through the discipline of celebration. We are all called to be women whose joy and optimism about the present spills over into hope and confidence for the future. This is our charge. When we accepted the good news, God guaranteed us comfort, bandages for broken hearts, garments of praise, and the oil of gladness.[31]

Our options are simple: We can be women who merely cope, or barely cope. Or we can be women who are so convinced of God's grace and goodness that we dare to face thoughts of the future with laughter.

It is a less-than-cordial world we face every morning. Obstacles to joy erupt at every turn. The discipline of celebration calls all of us to lighthearted living in spite of personal circumstances, national or international fears and uncertainties. As

Christ's beloved, we are always enfolded in his arms. His resources are always open to us; his power is always at work on our behalf. Our safety, in the present, as well as in the future, lies in his abiding love.

John Piper wrote:

> God's heart is not divided toward you. If you belong to Christ by faith, then everything God could possibly give you for your good he has signed over to your account in Christ. You hear the same answer at every point: Is this promise in my account? Yes. Is this blessing in my account? Yes. Yes. Yes. All the promises of God are Yes in Christ. Christ is God's Yes to all future grace.[32]

If we have Christ, we have God's "Yes." We have his assurance that he will be sufficient for whatever awaits us—today, next week, and next year. We can live free of paralyzing fear and heart-dragging pessimism because Jesus holds our lives in tender hands. His presence is our joy and our confidence. In spite of uncertainties and chaos and catastrophe, we can live among our friends and family with humor and playfulness because we have confidence in "future grace."

As the beloved bride of Christ, we can know that all of our tomorrows are secure. We don't have any reason for dread. We are held in the arms of one whose greatest joy is to lavish his love on us. We have good reason to smile today, and to laugh outright as we joyfully contemplate God's care for us in the days to come.

Celebrating the Smile of God

Dr. Sherwood "Woody" Wirt was my first writing mentor. The editor of Billy Graham's *Decision* magazine for nearly thirty years, he is the author of twenty-eight books and countless magazine articles. His book, *The God Who Smiles*, recently arrived in bookstores joining *Jesus, Man of Joy* as his latest works. As soon as I saw it I e-mailed him my congratulations.

"I'm almost ninety now, you know," he answered. "These are probably my final works."

The thought of it saddens me, but if they are, his last words may be his finest. He has stared long into the face of God and given us a word picture of what he has seen. Now with these books, he leaves us this legacy: a portrait of a smiling Father and Son. Once again, Woody becomes my mentor.

I want to be so preoccupied with the smile of God, so aware of his eternal joy, that as every year passes I become more and more convinced of reasons to celebrate. I want to be so sure of my inheritance in Christ that I get up every morning determined to face the day with a light heart.

"The LORD is good," wrote the psalmist.[33] Our little English word *good* doesn't even come close to expressing what the Hebrew writer meant. It takes a whole passel of words in the Hebrew lexicon to give us an idea of what the Old Testament writer wanted to convey about God. Here are just a few: pleasant, beautiful, excellent, lovely, delightful, precious, kind, righteous, *joyful*, and *cheerful*.

This is the God who is deserving of our worship. He calls us to live in the light of his goodness with celebratory hearts.

"Don't be troubled"—some of the last words Jesus said to his followers; "Do not be anxious about anything," added the apostle Paul. As children of God, gladness is our heritage. Joy is coded into our spiritual DNA. We are destined for celebration, and it can begin here and now.

God Is All Right

George MacDonald wrote:

> Friends, let us arise and live—arise even in the darkest
> moments of spiritual stupidity, when hope itself sees nothing
> to hope for. Let us go at once to the Life. Let us comfort our-
> selves in the thought of the Father and the Son. So long as
> there dwells harmony, so long as the Son loves the Father with
> all the love the Father can welcome, all is well with us, His lit-
> tle ones. God is all right. Why should we mind standing in the
> dark for a minute outside His window?[34]

It is often dark here, outside of heaven—dark and dangerous
and scary. *But God is all right.* Nothing can overpower his sovereign goodness and omnipotence. Wars may rage, nations may be
destroyed, but the kingdom of God will never be harmed, his
throne never toppled.

God will reign, as he always has. He will shower his grace
down on us, pour it into us, soak us in it, and send us soaring in
the strength of it. His will cannot be thwarted, and his love cannot be dimmed. His arms are around us, his breath close enough
to sweeten the air we breathe.

He is not frightened by the massive cumulative evil on this
planet. He is not overwhelmed by the horrors of the past, or the
ones that might yet happen.

Nuclear capabilities don't alarm God.

War strategies don't confuse or upset him.

Outbreaks of disease don't panic him.

Today's disasters don't trouble him, and tomorrow's threats
don't distress him.

Through the discipline of worship we say with our lives that God is worthy of our trust, he is deserving of our obedience and love. We declare that he is the loving, compassionate Friend of sinners.

Exercising the discipline of celebration, we say it all with a smile.

12

~

LIVING IN THE REALITY
OF THE INVISIBLE

*O*ne of the most significant moments of spiritual understanding occurred for me while I was doing the most common, mundane task. I was on my hands and knees, wiping muddy
paw prints off the foyer tile, when I was suddenly struck with the
incongruity of my life. Only moments earlier I had been engaged
with Omnipotence in quiet prayer. In the next, I was bending
and scrubbing, struggling to figure out how to translate the truth
of my belovedness into the experience of "real life."

I felt distant from the reality that I am the bride of Christ.
Then, in a moment of radiant clarity, it came to me that the ultimate challenge for me as a believer is this: to learn to live in the
reality of the invisible.

That's what the writer of Hebrews had in mind when he
wrote, "Now faith is being sure of what we hope for and certain
of what we do not see."[1]

It is what Paul was saying when he wrote, "So we fix our eyes
not on what is seen, but on what is unseen. For what is seen is
temporary, but what is unseen is eternal."[2]

It has been many years since that day on my knees on a muddy foyer, but when I think about turning points in my spiritual life, it is among my most poignant memories. It was the beginning of great confusion and a diligent searching. I desperately wanted to understand how to make the invisible truths of my faith concrete realities.

Patiently, kindly, over a period of years, God began to teach me that it is through the exercise of the spiritual disciplines that the invisible realities become real to us. I will always be deeply grateful for the gentle way he handled me at a time when I was in great need of firsthand, experiential knowledge of his heart and of his goodwill toward me.

Making the connection between the spiritual disciplines and my love of riding was for me a huge step away from the legalism of my faith. It was one of the sweetest acts of God toward me— using something I enjoyed, something that brought me great pleasure, to give me a picture of discipleship and an understanding of the function of the disciplines in a context of enjoyment and purpose. He used the simple, crude metaphor of riding to help me understand that the disciplines are spiritual activities undertaken with the physical body and used by God to lovingly lead us into the comfort and joy of knowing him.

As I've wrestled with my inadequacies, God has taught me that it is not important that I perform the disciplines perfectly at all times, but that "a naked intent toward God, the desire for Him alone, is enough."[3] How different that is from the earlier intent of my spiritual life. As a young Christian, I desired to live a good life and do good things. I desired acceptance and approval and a clear conscience before God and before men and women. But desiring God himself, alone, above everything? It had never occurred to me.

Only when I had grown exhausted with the doing did I begin to consider the idea that maybe, just maybe, God had something more in mind for me, something more meaningful, more satisfying than checking items off of a spiritual to-do list.

For every Christian, there must come a time when we realize that, for all our knowing about God, we don't really know *him* at all. We begin to feel a thirst that we can't quench by simply reading a verse or two in the Bible. A quick prayer at mealtime doesn't satisfy a gnawing hunger in our spirits that lingers long after we leave the table.

If we are fortunate, we have contact with one or two Christians whose lives resonate with the presence of Christ, and we are, quite frankly, baffled by them. Then, as though gently shaken from a light sleep, we become aware that, for all our doing right, we haven't gotten it right at all. What God wants is for us to know him, like one lover knows another. And we realize that all we know is how to act; we don't know how to love.

The realization astounds us. But before we can claim credit for figuring out the mystery, God assures us that this is his doing. It is God who is at work within us, both to will and to do his good pleasure.[4]

John of the Cross wrote, "It is not of your doing at all, this moment when your soul awakens. He creates in you the desire to find Him and run after Him—to follow where He leads you, and to press peacefully against His heart wherever He is."[5]

It is at this point that the spiritual disciplines have significance. They mark the route we take as we run after God. They lead us along the path that takes us into intimacy. They become our compass and chart into the invisible realities of the kingdom of God.

All these activities that we call spiritual disciplines train us who are flawed and finite to know God, who is holy and infinite. They lead us into ever-deepening levels of intimacy with him, where we discover new canyons of grace and love. They train us to live in the reality of the invisible.

Where to Begin

Teresa of Avila wrote, "The Lord told me to get started as best I could, that afterward I would see what His Majesty could do. And how well I have seen it."[6]

I take great comfort in the words of this saintly woman. "Just get started somewhere," she was saying. "Begin."

Marie began with prayer and study. After a lifetime of being on the outside, yearning for intimacy with God, she determined, with God's help, to get to know him, to abide in him. She determined to learn about his love, to live in the reality of that love. She started reading verses in Psalms, writing down her responses to the verses and her needs. And then she prayed.

Marie was incredulous as she told me, "I started praying fifteen minutes a day. Now I'm praying longer, about many more things, and God is, well, he's just amazing!"

We were chatting over coffee at a little bistro in the mall, and as I listened to her account of answers to prayer, I thought, *Lord, you're dazzling her with your love!* It is love that would never have been recognizable to her had she not *begun* with God, through a spiritual discipline.

"So many things, Jan," she said, smiling and shaking her head, "only God could have done them! One by one, he's taken care of everything I've needed—a job, an apartment—just when I needed them. I never imagined God would care so much and do so much for me."

Marie is seeing what his majesty will do when his beloved ones follow where he leads and press against his heart.

Although I've pursued intimacy with God for many years, often there are days when I feel as though I am just beginning to get to know him. Many days I get up and, engulfed by confusion, I think, *What's it all about? How do I live out what I believe today? How do I relate to you, God? How can I experience you, who are invisible, infinite, glorious?*

I feel awkward, clumsy in the presence of royalty. I have to make myself sit still and visualize the King drawing his bride into a private chamber to sit alone with her and reassure her of his love, his commitment, his tender concern for her. For me to "begin" means being silent before God to hear his love words. It means being reminded that I am his, and he loves me deeply, absolutely.

It means shaking off old thought patterns that would send me into a frenzy of legalistic tasks. It means recalling that Jesus is my Lover, my King, and that interacting with him is the way to intimacy with him. It means remembering that when Jesus said "Abide in me," he wasn't telling us to follow a list of strict rules and regulations; he was saying, "Live with me, share my life—get to know me!"

George MacDonald wrote, "The whole secret of progress is doing the thing we know. There is no other way of progress in the spiritual life, no other way of progress in the understanding of that life. Only as we do can we know."[7]

The starting place is always here, always now. We begin by doing what we know—prayer, meditation, service—whatever activity God's Holy Spirit is drawing us to share with the King. And there, in that place, engaged with Omnipotence, we gain understanding. We gain new knowledge of the love of God, and we plant the seeds of intimacy.

Failures and Setbacks

We've all heard how important it is to get back into the saddle after you've fallen off a horse. It's a metaphor used for many life experiences, but I learned how true it was when I was riding every day. Falls were part of the learning curve, and getting back up wasn't something a teacher or trainer would negotiate. You just did it.

You always began again where you fell, at the fence where your horse "ran out" or "refused," where you lost concentration and went off course, or where you shifted your weight and sent the wrong message to your mount. You didn't go back to the starting gate. You picked up at the place where the problem occurred, where you got lazy, or where you misjudged the distance. You made the correction there, where you had trouble.

For us who want to walk with God, who want to move into deeper levels of intimacy with him, "falls" are going to be common. For too many of us, failure will send us into a tailspin. We'll think we've blown it so badly we have to go back to the "starting gate" and begin all over again. We'll feel so overwhelmed by the crash we'll seriously consider quitting altogether.

This is where I often find myself. This is the mind-set Henri Nouwen was addressing when he wrote about spiritual failure—those times when we fall and despair because we think we've lost all that was gained, and we're suddenly right back where we started. Not so, he wrote: "Try to think about it instead as being pulled off the road for a while. When you return to the road you return to the place where you left it, not to where you started."[8]

We will fail. Even after we have committed ourselves to exercising the spiritual disciplines in order to know God and experience him, we will be "pulled off the road."

We will succumb to human frailty and put off prayer. We will allow ourselves to become busy with things that take us away from study and solitude and service.

In the pursuit of other comforts, we will relegate intimacy with God to a lesser place and suddenly find our hearts cold toward him.

Then we will scold and beat up on ourselves and wonder how God could ever love us and accept us again. But in truth, he is standing right there, at the place where we left off following, and all we have to do is rush into his arms and humbly confess the truth of our condition: that he is our life and our strength and salvation.

How hard that will be for many of us. Legalism, false doctrine, and the rule of our own sin-scarred nature have conditioned us. We imagine God standing ready, waiting to bludgeon us with heart-bruising words of condemnation. How desperately we need to know that "our courteous Lord does not want his servants to despair because they fall often and grievously; for our failing does not hinder Him in loving us."[9]

Jesus gave us the parable of the prodigal son to illustrate the Lord's heart toward us when we have wandered away and squandered his love gifts. The Gospels tell us of Peter's denial and show us the way Jesus restored him: gently, kindly, fully. Throughout the record of Jesus' life we see only demons running from him in fear, never repentant sinners—these flocked to him! Stephen Charnock wrote: "He is the true Father, who has a quicker pace in meeting, than the prodigal in returning . . . because 'He delights in mercy'; He delights in the expression of it from Himself, and the acceptance of it by His creatures."[10]

Oh, that we could get in our minds the indelible image of a tender, compassionate Lord!

Brennan Manning asked, "Has the thunder of 'God loved the world so much' been so muffled by the roar of religious rhetoric that we are deaf to the word that God could have tender feelings for us?"[11]

Once, when our children were very small, Ken and I had to take a business trip. We had no family close by so we hired a baby-sitter to stay with Matt and Molly for several days. I'll never forget the moment we arrived home. Molly threw herself into my arms and blurted, "I broke the cake plate, Mommy, and *she* tried to make me pick up the pieces of glass. I wouldn't do it, and she got real mad, but I told her you never let me touch the glass. You always say, 'People are more important than things,' and you hug me and you touch the glass so I don't get cut."

The baby-sitter, for all her skill, was a hireling, not a parent. She had rules for enforcing, but no compassion to offer. Her response to a clumsy child was to shame her and punish her.

Why do we think that if we live clumsily amid the noble majesty of God that he will reject us and refuse to have anything more to do with us? That, like a hireling, he will leave us to clean up our own messes, with no thought to the danger to our souls?

Julian of Norwich wrote:

> For this passing life does not require us to live wholly without sin. He loves us endlessly, and we sin customarily, and He reveals it to us most gently. And then we sorrow and moan discreetly, turning to contemplate His mercy, cleaving to His love and to His goodness, seeing that He is our medicine, knowing that we only sin.[12]

Burn this into your heart: if we embark on a journey into intimacy with God, via the path marked by the spiritual disciplines, we will make huge and nasty messes along the way. But our failures don't alter the nature of God who loves us even in the face of our sins—not in spite of them, but in full view of them. Our weaknesses don't lessen the degree of his love for us.

I love the story of the desert fathers who went to one of their elders and asked what they should do if they caught a brother dozing during services. "Should we pinch him?" they asked.

The elder answered, "Actually, if I saw a brother sleeping, I would put his head on my knees and let him rest."[13]

What can we do to rid our minds of the idea that God is harsh with his children? That he is waiting to "pinch" us when we are weak? Of all the things most hurtful to God, surely it must be the way we slander him with our false impressions about the nature of his love for us. How often do we tell ourselves, and teach others, with our actions and our words, that God is not sympathetic with our weaknesses; that he is not patient and compassionate with us in our humanity; that when we fail him he is furious with us and unwilling to keep company with such as we?

Why are we so hard on ourselves, and others, when our lives are less than perfect and our hearts grow weary of trusting?

Madame Guyon, a woman of great faith, wrote this: "If you dare the spiritual pilgrimage, you need to remember in times of calamity, and in times of what appear to be dry spells, and in that time which men will call a spiritual winter: Life is there."[14]

Jesus is there. He is the life. Nothing will ever deflect his love away from us. Nothing we could ever do, or not do, will cause him to wash his hands of us.

It is no small thing that Paul told us: nothing will be able to separate us from the love of God that is in Christ Jesus our Lord.[15] This is our consolation. This is our reason for living. This is our reason for getting up when we have fallen.

We know that we are weak—"that we cannot stand for the twinkling of an eye, except with the protection of grace, and let us reverently cling to God, trusting only in Him."[16]

This is where we begin.

This is where we begin again.

Finding Welcome

"Abide with me," Jesus said. "Remain in me. Don't live on the outskirts of intimacy. Move in!"

The offer is staggering, really. "Everything Jesus is saying to you can be summarized in the words 'Know that you are welcome.' Jesus offers you his own most intimate life with the Father. He wants you to know all He knows and to do all He does. He wants His home to be yours."[17]

It is a magnificent gesture of generosity and acceptance, and yes, optimism, to open your home and invite someone to move in and live with you. Recently I heard about a young woman whose roommate came home drunk and began thrashing about the house, menacing everything within arm's length. Terrified, my young friend left quickly, but not before packing up a few valuables she feared might be destroyed by the rampaging roommate.

When we move into the place of intimacy with Christ, we are the ones who bring the element of risk into the relationship. We are the ones whose lives are unstable, undisciplined, clumsy, rude; we are the ones likely to bring havoc onto the scene. It is God who takes the great risk when he invites us to share his life, when he makes his offer of welcome.

The Father has adopted us, the Son made us his betrothed, but we've spent our lives on the streets and in the gutters. The life God offers us now, in this new relationship, is unfamiliar to us. We have been spiritual orphans living in poverty. We don't have any experience relating to this God who is now our Father; to this King who has made us his bride.

But God, in an unprecedented display of extravagant grace, opens his home to us. He invites us, the dysfunctional, the dispossessed, the displaced, and the disposable, to move right in with him. Bringing home the bums and the bag ladies, Jesus tells all of us, *"Mi casa es su casa."*

We can live with him, abiding with him through the exercise of the spiritual disciplines, learning what intimacy with a King is all about, or we can live at a distance and ache with longing.

We can accept his welcome, or we can wish for the warmth of intimacy.

The choice is ours; the risks God's.

Moving into Intimacy

Missionary friends told me the story about a young Nigerian man who fell deeply in love with a woman in his village. The young man's father negotiated the "bride price" with the girl's father, and the wedding celebration was planned. Not a stingy man, the groom's father hosted a lavish party and served all the guests Coca-Cola.

The bride, however, was not so generous. In the early weeks after the marriage, her crass behavior devastated the young man. As though wanting to demonstrate her disdain for her husband, she slaughtered and cooked a chicken, in full view of the village, and ate the entire portion herself, saving none for him, offering none to her neighbors.

Shamed by his wife's boorish actions, the young man was

heartbroken. He asked the missionaries to pray with him that God would help him show his wife how much he loved her. It was a slow journey, made difficult and miserable at times by the woman's stubborn, selfish will, but over time, her husband's love won her.

I see myself in this story. A poor risk, I often leave God open to shame and embarrassment. Though he claims me as his bride, I often live at a distance, selfishly pursuing my own interests, my own passions, heedless of the yearning of his heart. But he has generously given me all that is his. He continues to offer me his forgiveness and companionship. He continues to desire intimacy with me.

It floors me. Why would God want me? Why would he pay such a high price to establish a relationship with me?

In my human reasoning, it would have been enough—more than enough—for Jesus simply to rescue me. Like a divine Lifeguard, he could have pulled me from the riptide, hauled me onto the beach, administered CPR, and then left me to the mercy of sun and sand. But that wouldn't have been enough for him. Having rescued me, he could do nothing less than take me home with him and give me a whole new life as his bride.

You see, Jesus doesn't consider himself a Lifeguard. He calls himself a Husband.[18]

The divine story is not a news report of a victim rescued by a mysterious stranger. It is a story of family love—a Father's for his children, a Husband's for his bride. And anything less than "happily ever after" would never satisfy the Author's intent.

God loves you. He loves me. "How great is the love the Father has lavished on us, that we should be called children of God!"[19]

How hard it is to see ourselves as the beloved children of the

Father and as the spotless bride of the Son. Unless the Holy Spirit opens our eyes and makes us aware of this profound truth, we see ourselves as unworthy, unloved, and unlovable. Yet "within us lies something incomparably more precious than what we see outside ourselves. Let's not imagine we are hollow inside."[20]

Inside us, in what was once a God-shaped vacuum, the very Spirit of God resides. His presence gives us immeasurable value. The gifts he brings with him make us the physical repositories of glory and grace. We are no longer bag ladies—we are royal heirs of the wealth of heaven and the beloved bride of the King of kings.

Will we put away our selfishness, our pride, our raging independence, and move into intimacy with him?

Getting in on Everything!

If I agree to live with him, on his terms, in the intimate way God desires, will he make good on his promises? Will what I gain be worth what I leave behind? Will God be equal to my faith?

Listen again to George MacDonald: "One day we shall laugh ourselves to scorn that we looked for so little from Thee, for thy giving will not be limited by our hoping."[21]

Imagine! My hoping—puny, finite, often undefined—cannot limit God's infinite giving. "The Father loves the Son extravagantly. He turned everything over to Him so He could give it away—a lavish distribution of gifts. That is why whoever accepts and trusts the Son gets in on everything."[22]

This is an astounding truth—that God wants to give us everything the Son enjoys: the beauty and perfection of heaven, the joy of intimate fellowship within the Trinity, the bliss of a holy, eternal union with his beloved (that's us!), and infinite gifts and pleasures we have not even thought to wish for! It's all ours, in Christ. It's ours by faith. We enjoy and experience it all here and now, in a limited manner because of our finite humanity— yet we possess it all now and enjoy it through the shared activities we call "spiritual disciplines."

How sad, how desperately sad, to mistake these disciplines for rules of behavior that will earn us favor with God. How sad to think we might put rules into effect in our lives, and in others' lives, with the hope that God won't "pinch" us. How sad to think that obeying them makes us good, or at least better than those who don't follow any rules at all. If this is our attitude toward the spiritual disciplines, we are destined for spiritual confusion and the tightfisted grip of legalism. We will be baffled by the joy we see in others whose hearts have found rest in the love of God.

Being God's

Throughout the months of writing this book, I spent time with many different Christians, at many different age levels in their faith. Most knew little, if anything, about the spiritual disciplines, except for those four or five disciplines their respective churches encouraged. One, a pastor, knew quite a lot, but he expressed concern about a book that would encourage Christians to exercise the spiritual disciplines. "Folks need to beware of making the disciplines an end in themselves," he warned me. "Our identity in Christ and our union with Christ drive our pursuit of him through the disciplines."

My point exactly.

"Some Christians turn the disciplines into a formula—if you do these disciplines you therefore are spiritual."

No, that's not what I wanted to say.

"Frankly, I've observed plenty of stone-cold, well-disciplined Christians."

He articulated the one great fear that haunted me during the writing of this book: that the sweet, welcoming message of "Be God's!" would be shouted down by the shrill and unkind voice we all hear that yells at us to "Be good!" If that message has insinuated itself into even one page of this book, I have failed.

If, in studying the spiritual disciplines, we miss the message that God made us for himself, and nothing we crave, nothing we yearn for apart from him will ever satisfy us—not showy good works, not first-class performance, not even quiet, steady niceness—then the truth has eluded us.

Nothing is a substitute for knowing God and experiencing intimacy with him.

"Nothing is noble enough for the desire of the heart of man but oneness with the eternal. For this, God must make him yield his very being, that God may enter in and dwell with him."[23]

A Deep Paradox

The challenge is in the yielding. "Everything involves struggle before the habit is acquired. Nothing is learned without a little effort."[24] This is what Paul was saying when he wrote, "Continue to work out your salvation with fear and trembling."[25] But in the next breath he added that it is God who is working in us to incline our hearts toward God, to desire God's purposes, not our own.

In the final analysis, we can say only it is all of God—the craving to know him originates with him and the impetus to exercise any discipline that draws us into deeper levels of intimacy with him derives from his Spirit.

"It is a relief to know that the life of discipleship is never something merely learned—not even through hard and painful struggle. Rather it is a continually new experience of grace. What a deep paradox!"[26]

John of the Cross expressed that paradox still more poignantly with these words: "If you are seeking after God, you may be sure of this: God is seeking you much more. He is the Lover, and you are His beloved. He has promised Himself to you."[27]

God's Provision for the Journey

The duke and duchess of Windsor once visited Virginia's luxurious Homestead resort where they indulged in every expensive pleasure available. When a hotel clerk presented the duke with a bill at checkout, the duke stared at it, puzzled. "What do I do with this?" he asked. "I'm not used to paying bills."

It's not easy for us to relate to that kind of wealth. Most of us live on a budget. Few of us can imagine embarking on a journey with no thought of the cost. We can't fathom what it would be like to be royalty, to travel at the king's expense and never have to worry about paying the bill.

But if we have set our hearts on pilgrimage, if we have determined, through the leading of God's Holy Spirit, to walk with God, to travel into deeper levels of intimacy with him, living out the reality of his invisible kingdom, God himself will handle the bill. He will ensure that we have everything we need to make the journey. "My God will meet all your needs according to his glorious riches in Christ Jesus," Paul wrote.[28]

Teresa of Avila said this: "It is a great thing to have experienced the friendship and favor He shows toward those who journey on this road and how He takes care of almost all the expenses."[29]

Our cost: the cost of saying no to self. This is the truest definition of discipline, but in saying no to self, we are saying yes to God. We are saying yes to the one thing that our souls desire above everything—a life of intimacy and friendship with almighty God.

We are saying yes to a journey that will take us where no other path can lead—into a deep and meaningful relationship with God; into the knowledge of the mystery of God, "namely, Christ, in whom are hidden all the treasures of wisdom and knowledge."[30]

It is a journey to the only place our souls will ever call home. May it begin here, now.

Intimate Faith

A Study Guide

CHAPTER 1: DABBLERS OR DISCIPLES?

1. In your experience, what disciplines are most familiar, most frequently practiced? Which are least familiar?

2. Describe your experience with the practice of spiritual disciplines.

3. What do you see as their function in the life of faith?

4. Read Isaiah 29:13 and consider what misconceptions you might need to address regarding the exercise of the spiritual disciplines.

5. Consider the statement that "it is through discipline that grace is best experienced." How might this be true in your life?

CHAPTER 2: "MY LIFE IS IN YOUR HANDS"

1. How does the exercise of humility and submission affect your response to a sovereign God?

2. How would you reconcile the exercise of humility with issues of self-esteem and the need to feel significant?

3. What do you see as some practical examples of godly humility within the family? Within the Body of Christ?

4. How do you see the exercise of humility preparing you for practicing other spiritual disciplines?

5. What are some specific areas of bondage from which the exercise of humility and submission can offer you freedom?

CHAPTER 3: BROODING ON THE SCRIPTURE

1. How would you characterize your practice of the discipline of study?

2. What is your primary motive for studying the Bible?

3. How does the Bible's theme of romance affect your attitude toward study?

4. Legalism always haunts a discussion of discipline. Regarding study, how might Romans 8:1 speak grace to your heart?

5. What changes might you consider making so that the discipline of study is more meaningful for you?

CHAPTER 4: ASSEMBLING A LIFE BEFORE GOD

1. What emotions are triggered for you by a discussion of the discipline of sacrifice?

2. How do you see freedom expressed through the exercise of simplicity and sacrifice?

3. Under what circumstances have you yearned for simplicity?

4. Under what circumstances have you sensed God calling you to exercise the discipline of sacrifice? What was your response?

5. Have you ever "sawed off the limb on which you're sitting"? How did God break your fall?

6. How do you see the disciplines of simplicity and sacrifice making you "ready for anything"?

CHAPTER 5: LIVING IN ANTICIPATION

1. How significant is fasting to your spiritual life?

2. What circumstances would motivate you to fast? What would you expect from God in response?

3. What does it mean to you to know that Jesus is fasting and praying for you at this moment?

4. Why do you think deep love for God is so vital to the practice of chastity?

5. Why do you think chastity is such a huge challenge to the human spirit?

6. Lamentations 3:22–23 reinforces the idea of "second chances," or "regained chastity." How does this affect you? How does it affect your attitude toward others?

7. How can the exercise of fasting and chastity cultivate anticipation for Christ as the Bridegroom?

CHAPTER 6: CONTENT WITH HIDDENNESS

1. What obstacles to discipleship does secrecy address?

2. How do you see the discipline of secrecy cultivating intimacy with God in fasting? In prayer? In service?

3. In what way does the exercise of secrecy cultivate contentment in God?

4. In what ways can the exercise of the discipline of secrecy affect your relationship with others at home? At work? Within the Body of Christ?

5. How does the idea that God values secrecy affect your response to Him?

CHAPTER 7: THE GREAT ENCOUNTER

1. What has been your experience with the discipline of stillness?

2. What does Jesus' exercise of solitude reveal about him?

3. What changes would you have to make in order to make the discipline of solitude a life habit? What would you expect from God in response?

4. What challenge does the discipline of silence pose for you? Before God? Before others?

5. How do you see the disciplines of stillness as the "great encounter from which all other encounters derive their meaning"?

CHAPTER 8: SANCTURY IN THE HEART OF GOD

1. What has been your experience with the discipline of meditation? What misconceptions about this discipline do you need to address?

2. How might the exercise of meditation be a defense against "mischief"? How do you see it cultivating faith and love for God?

3. Why do you think prayer is so vital to the life of faith?

4. What does the statement "Prayer is about a relationship, not a wish list" mean to you?

5. What significance do you see in the fact that Jesus' disciples asked him to teach them to pray?

6. How does an understanding of the sovereignty of God and the exercise of humility affect your prayer life? Your response to God's answers to your prayers?

CHAPTER 9: LOVE IN ACTION

1. How do you see service, in general terms, as an evidence of God's imprint on His creation?

2. Under what circumstances does service become a spiritual discipline?

3. Why do you think it is dangerous to try to exercise the discipline of service apart from the exercise of other disciplines, such as humility, worship, secrecy?

4. The discipline of service requires us to prioritize wisely. What changes do you need to make in order to exercise service that meets the biblical imperative to take care of "first things first"?

5. What do you think is meant by the statement that "the basin is the way of blessing"?

CHAPTER 10: LIFE IN PROFOUND CONJUNCTION

1. How do you think the life of faith is diminished when fellowship is lacking? How is it enhanced?

2. How do you see the theology of the Trinity as important to your understanding of the exercise of the discipline of fellowship?

3. In what ways have you experienced the truth of the statement that "a good means of having God is to speak with his friends"?

4. In what way did Jesus exercise the discipline of confession?

5. How is confession essential to our relationship with God? With others?

6. What other disciplines do you see as essential to the practice of confession before God? Before others?

CHAPTER 11: THE DELIGHT OF HEAVEN

1. What are some of the most poignant times of worship you have experienced?

2. Why do you think the discipline of sacrifice is so important to the exercise of the discipline of worship?

3. How do you see the other disciplines, in addition to sacrifice, giving worship its shape and expression?

4. What are some practical ways you can cultivate a life of worship?

5. When is celebration a discipline?

6. How does your exercise of the discipline of celebration reveal the level of trust and confidence you have in God's sovereign goodness and love?

7. What would it look like to you to be "a woman who can laugh at the days to come" (Prov. 31:25b)?

CHAPTER 12: LIVING IN THE REALITY OF THE INVISIBLE

1. How do you see the practice of the spiritual disciplines as tools for teaching you to "live in the reality of the invisible truths of God and His kingdom"?

2. Why can't we take credit for any sense of yearning we feel for God, for intimacy with Him?

3. In what way does the practice of the spiritual disciplines give us concrete, tangible ways of responding to Christ's call to "abide in Me"?

4. How does the theology of grace beckon us to "begin with Christ"?

5. What does it mean to you to think of God as the Father who *ran* to meet the prodigal son? Can you believe that God is running toward you now, anxious to welcome you into intimacy with Him?

6. Consider the phrase "living on the outskirts of intimacy." What changes do you need to make in your life to begin moving toward God?

7. God has promised to "meet all your needs according to His glorious riches in Christ Jesus" (Phil. 4:19). What does this mean to you as you consider the cost of discipleship?

8. In Christ "are hidden all the treasures of wisdom and knowledge" (Col. 2:2–3). He is "the way, the truth, and the life" (John 14:6). What is preventing you from pursuing Him with all your heart?

"Thanks be to God for His indescribable gift!"
2 Corinthians 9:15

NOTES

CHAPTER 1: DABBLERS OR DISCIPLES?

1. Brennan Manning, *Reflections for Ragamuffins* (New York: HarperCollins, 1998), 201.
2. Mariano DiGangi, ed., *A Golden Treasury of Puritan Devotion* (Phillipsburg, N.J.: P&R Publishing, 1999), 95.
3. Ibid., 19.
4. Henri Nouwen, *Life of the Beloved* (New York: Crossroad, 1992), 21.
5. Jeremiah 6:16.
6. Manning, *Reflections for Ragamuffins*, 330.
7. Thomas Merton, *Life and Holiness* (New York: Image Books, Doubleday, The Abbey of Gethsemani, Inc., 1963), 8.
8. I am deeply grateful to Dallas Willard's book, *The Spirit of the Disciplines* (NY: HarperCollins, 1988). His categorizing of the disciplines, i.e., the disciplines of abstinence, deepened and enriched my understanding of how God trains us to learn of his sufficiency in all things.
9. John Piper, *Desiring God* (Sisters, Ore.: Multnomah Books, 1986), 50.
10. Gary Thomas, *Seeking the Face of God* (Eugene, Ore.: Harvest House Publishers, 1994), 234.
11. Ephesians 1:18–19.
12. Matthew 28:20.
13. Jean-Pierre deCaussade, *The Sacrament of the Present Moment* trans. Kitty Muggeridge (New York: HarperCollins, 1989), xiii.

14. Oswald Chambers, *My Utmost for His Highest* (New York: Dodd, Mead & Company, 1935), 19.
15. DiGangi, *Golden Treasury of Puritan Devotion*, 13.

CHAPTER 2: "MY LIFE IS IN YOUR HANDS"

1. Sam Negri, "The Last of the Old-Time Traders," *Arizona Highways*, January 1997, Vol. 73, No. 1, p. 4.
2. C. S. Lewis, *Letters to Malcolm: Chiefly on Prayer* (New York: Harcourt Brace and World, 1963), 114.
3. Francois Fénelon, *Francois Fénelon*, trans. Mildred Whitney Stillman (Minneapolis: Bethany House, 1975), 205.
4. From Isaiah 46:9–11, author's paraphrase.
5. DeCaussade, *Sacrament of the Present Moment*, 11.
6. John Eldredge, *The Journey of Desire* (Nashville: Thomas Nelson, 2000), 180.
7. Philip Yancey, *Reaching for the Invisible God* (Grand Rapids: Zondervan Publishing House, 2000), 273.
8. From Psalm 139:1–4, author's paraphrase.
9. Charles Bridges, *Psalm 119: A Commentary* (Edinburgh: Banner of Truth Trust, 1974), 201.
10. Ibid, 175.
11. Ephesians 5:21.
12. Proverbs 14:7 NASB.
13. Richard Foster, *The Celebration of Discipline* (New York: HarperCollins, 1978), 117.
14. Ibid., 113.
15. Philippians 2:5–7.
16. Charles Ringma, *Dare to Journey with Henri Nouwen* (Colorado Springs: Piñon Press, 2000), Reflection 9.
17. Tessa Bielecki, *Teresa of Avila: Ecstasy and Common Sense* (Boston: Shambhala Publications, Inc., 1996), 5.

18. François Fénelon, *Meditations on the Heart of God*, trans. Robert J. Edmonson (Brewster, Mass.: Paraclete Press, 1997), 141.

19. Ibid., 112.

20. George MacDonald, *Knowing the Heart of God*, comp. Michael Phillips (Minneapolis: Bethany House Publishers, 1990), 205.

CHAPTER 3: BROODING ON THE SCRIPTURE

1. A. W. Tozer, *That Incredible Christian* (Harrisburg, Pa.: Christian Publications, Inc., 1964), 137.

2. Eldredge, *Journey of Desire*, 203–4.

3. Ibid, 203.

4. John 1:3, author's paraphrase.

5. Henri Nouwen, *With Burning Hearts* (Maryknoll, N.Y.: Orbis Books, 1994), 48.

6. 2 Timothy 3:17 MSG.

7. 1 Corinthians 2:9–10.

8. Eugene Peterson, *Living the Message* (NY: HarperCollins, 1996), 316.

9. John Piper, *A Godward Life*, vol. 2 (Sisters, Ore.: Multnomah Publishers, 1999), 182.

10. Bridges, *Psalm 119: A Commentary*, 13.

11. John Piper, *God's Passion for His Glory* (Wheaton: Crossway Books, 1998), 75.

12. Nouwen, *With Burning Hearts*, 46–7.

13. Psalm 62:11–12.

CHAPTER 4: ASSEMBLING A LIFE BEFORE GOD

1. Eugene Peterson, *Living the Message* (New York: HarperCollins Publishers, 1996), 164.

2. Ibid., 49.

3. Mark 6:8–9.
4. Lamentations 3:23.
5. Matthew 6:25–26.
6. George MacDonald, *An Anthology*, ed. C. S. Lewis (New York: MacMillan Publishing Company, 1947), 33.
7. Philippians 3:13–14.
8. Brother Lawrence, *Practicing His Presence* (Augusta, Maine: Christian Books, 1973), 45.
9. Calvin Miller, *The Unchained Soul* (Minneapolis: Bethany House Publishers, 1995), 39.
10. Dallas Willard, *The Spirit of the Disciplines* (New York: HarperCollins, 1988), 175.
11. Ibid.
12. Chambers, *My Utmost for His Highest*, 300.
13. Thomas, *Seeking the Face of God*, 115.
14. 1 Corinthians 13:5 KJV.
15. Ephesians 6:15.
16. Piper, *Godward Life*, vol. 2, 285.
17. Psalm 119:26 KJV.

CHAPTER 5: LIVING IN ANTICIPATION

1. Matthew 9:15.
2. Piper, *Godward Life*, vol. 2, 192.
3. Jeremiah 14:12.
4. Psalm 51:17.
5. Brennan Manning, *The Ragamuffin Gospel* (Sisters, Ore.: Multnomah Publishers: 1990), 161.
6. See Mark 9:14–29.
7. Daniel 1:12, 10:3.
8. John 4:32.
9. Matthew 26:29.
10. Eldredge, *Journey of Desire*, 134.

11. Piper, *Godward Life II*, 192.
12. Willard, *Spirit of the Disciplines*, 172.
13. 1 Corinthians 7:3–6.
14. Psalm 37:5–6.
15. Piper, *Godward Life II*, 193.
16. See John 4:1–26.
17. See John 8:1–11.

CHAPTER 6: CONTENT WITH HIDDENNESS

1. Bridges, *Psalm 119*, 256.
2. Matthew 6:1, 3.
3. Foster, *Celebration of Discipline*, 128.
4. Matthew 6:2.
5. Dallas Willard, *The Divine Conspiracy* (New York: HarperCollins Publishers, 1998), 200.
6. Matthew 6:16.
7. Matthew 6:4, 6, 18.
8. Fénelon, *Meditations on the Heart of God*, 114.

CHAPTER 7: THE GREAT ENCOUNTER

1. Thomas, *Seeking the Face of God*, 104.
2. Psalm 46:10.
3. Psalm 37:7.
4. Luke 5:16.
5. Willard, *Spirit of the Disciplines*, ix.
6. John 5:19–20.
7. Modern Spirituality Series, *Henri Nouwen* (Springfield, Ill.: Templegate Publishers, 1988), 77.
8. Psalm 63:1 KJV.
9. Thomas, *Seeking the Face of God*, 53.

10. Brother Lawrence, *The Practice of the Presence of God*, ed. Harold J. Chadwick (North Brunswick, N.J.: Bridge-Logos Publishers, 1999), 94.
11. Psalm 51:17, MSG.
12. Modern Spirituality Series, *Nouwen*, 77.
13. Leo Tolstoy, *A Calendar of Wisdom*, trans. Peter Sekirin (New York: Scribner, 1997), 246.
14. John Climacus, *The Ladder of Divine Ascent*, trans. Colm Luibheid and Norman Russell (New York: The Missionary Society of St. Paul the Apostle, 1982), 158.
15. Mother Teresa, *A Simple Path* (New York: Ballantine, 1995), 7.
16. Isaiah 30:15.
17. Psalm 62:5.
18. Psalm 88:1, 3, 9, 14.
19. James 1:19.
20. Calvin Miller, *Into the Depths of God* (Minneapolis: Bethany House Publishers, 2000), 119.
21. Proverbs 10:19.
22. Proverbs 21:23.
23. Faith Hill, *Grace in Winter* (Edinburgh: Banner of Truth Trust, 1989), 64.
24. Sam Johnson and Jan Winebrenner, *Captive Warriors* (College Station: Texas A&M University Press, 1988), 139.
25. Peterson, *Living the Message*, 36.
26. Brennan Manning, *Abba's Child* (Colorado Springs: NavPress, 1994), 64.

CHAPTER 8: SANCTURY IN THE HEART OF GOD

1. Foster, *Celebration of Discipline*, 20.
2. Psalm 119:27.
3. Psalm 119:23 KJV.
4. Psalm 8:3.

5. Psalm 16:8.
6. Psalm 19:10
7. Psalm 19:14
8. Philippians 4:8.
9. Philippians 1:21.
10. Brother Lawrence, *Practicing His Presence*, 48.
11. Hebrews 12:1.
12. 1 Corinthians 10:13.
13. Bridges, *Psalm 119*, 204 [emphasis in original].
14. Brother Lawrence, *Practice of the Presence of God*, 92.
15. William Johnston, ed., *The Cloud of Unknowing* (New York: Image Books, 1973), 47.
16. A. W. Tozer, *The Divine Conquest* (Wheaton: Tyndale House Publishers, Living Books, 1995), 7.
17. Marciano Di Gangi, ed. *A Golden Treasury of Puritan Devotion* (Phillipsburg, N.J.: P&R Publishing, 1995), 143.
18. Psalm 1:2, 3 MSG.
19. DeCaussade, *Sacrament of the Present Moment*, 2.
20. Psalm 17:6–7.
21. Psalm 18:6.
22. Psalm 5:3.
23. Psalm 6:9.
24. Psalm 20:6.
25. Teresa of Avila, *Life of Prayer*, ed. Dr. James M. Houston (Minneapolis: Bethany House Publishers, 1998), 52.
26. Psalm 18:35 KJV.
27. Walt Wangerin Jr., *Whole Prayer* (Grand Rapids: Zondervan Publishing House, 1998), 90.
28. Bielecki, *Teresa of Avila*, 5.
29. Andrew Murray, *With Christ in the School of Prayer* (Chicago: M.A. Donohue & Co.), 28.
30. Teresa of Avila, *Life of Prayer*, 52.
31. Wangerin Jr., *Whole Prayer*, 33.

32. Yancey, *Reaching for the Invisible God*, 169.
33. John 14:14.
34. Matthew 7:7 KJV.
35. James 4:3.
36. James 1:8
37. Philippians 4:19.
38. James 1:5.
39. 1 John 1:9.
40. Deuteronomy 31:8; Isaiah 41:10.
41. Romans 8:28.
42. John 3:16.
43. Miller, *Into the Depths of God*, 83.
44. Hebrews 4:16.
45. Matthew 7:7–11.
46. Philippians 4:6.
47. Peterson, *Living the Message*, 9.
48. MacDonald, *Knowing the Heart of God*, 205.
49. Teresa of Avila, *Life of Prayer*, 2.
50. Luke 11:1.
51. Peterson, *Living the Message*, 40–41.
52. George Müller, *Release the Power of Prayer* (New Kensington: Whitaker House, 1999), 28.
53. Ibid, 81.
54. François Fénelon, *Talking with God*, trans. Hal Helms (Brewster, Mass.: Paraclete Press, 1997), 11.
55. *The John Donne Treasury*, ed. by Erwin Paul Rudolph (Wheaton: Victor Books, SP Publications, 1978), 67.
56. Revelation 5:8.
57. Brent Curtis and John Eldredge, *The Sacred Romance: Drawing Closer to the Heart of God* (Nashville: Thomas Nelson, 1997).
58. Romans 8:34.
59. Romans 8:32.

60. John Piper, *Future Grace* (Sisters, Ore.: Multnomah Publishers, Inc., 1995), 117.
61. Ibid., 115.
62. Miller, *Into the Depths of God*, 84.
63. Piper, *Godward Life*, vol. 2, 304.
64. Jeremiah 12:5.

CHAPTER 9: LOVE IN ACTION

1. Genesis 1:26.
2. Willard, *Spirit of the Disciplines*, 182.
3. Ibid.
4. John 13:14–17.
5. Foster, *Celebration of Discipline*, 127.
6. Bielecki, *Teresa of Avila*, 14.
7. Luke 16:13.
8. Psalm 100:2 NASV.
9. Matt 6:1–3.
10. I Pet 5:5–6.
11. Rom 12:1 NASV.
12. Colossians 4:2–4.
13. *Dallas Morning News* April 21, 2001, 5G.
14. Brother Lawrence, *Practicing His Presence* (Augusta, Maine: Christian Books, 1973), 57.
15. 1 Corinthians 13:1, 3.
16. Bielecki, *Teresa of Avila*, 26.
17. Peterson, *Living the Message*, 230.
18. John and Linda Friel, *An Adult Child's Guide to What's Normal* (Deerfield Beach, Fla.: Health Communications Inc., 1990), 163.
19. Ringma, *Dare to Journey with Henri Nouwen*, Reflection 31.
20. Leviticus 19:18.
21. 1 Timothy 5:8.

22. Manning, *Abba's Child*, 169.
23. Matthew 11:28–29 MSG.
24. Fénelon, *Meditations on the Heart of God*, 73.
25. Dorothy L. Sayers, *Creed or Chaos?* (Manchester, N.H.: Sophia Institute Press, 1999), 26.
26. Amy Carmichael, *You Are My Hiding Place* (Minneapolis: Bethany House Publishers, 1991), 9.
27. John Eldredge, *Wild at Heart* (Nashville: Thomas Nelson Publishers, 2001), 203.
28. Isaiah 62:5.
29. Romans 16:1.
30. Hebrews 6:10.
31. 1 Timothy 3:13.
32. Isaiah 61:1–3

CHAPTER 10: LIFE IN PROFOUND CONJUNCTION

1. Willard, *Spirit of the Disciplines*, 187.
2. Eldredge, *Journey of Desire*, 139.
3. John 17:20–23, 26.
4. Bielecki, *Teresa of Avila*, 17.
5. Willard, *Spirit of the Disciplines*, 186.
6. Matthew 5:16 MSG.
7. Bielecki, *Teresa of Avila*, 17.
8. Matthew 20:26–28.
9. J. Heinrich Arnold, *Discipleship: Living for Christ in the Daily Grind* (Farmington, Pa.: The Plough Publishing House, 1994), 79.
10. 1 Corinthians 12:12, 21, 27.
11. Matthew 18:20.
12. George MacDonald, *Discovering the Character of God* (Minneapolis: Bethany House Publishers, 1989), 186.
13. Romans 7:19.
14. 1 John 1:9 NASB.

15. James 5:16.
16. 1 Peter 2:9.
17. Dietrich Bonhoeffer, *Life Together* (New York: Harper & Row, 1952), 116.
18. Wangerin Jr., *Whole Prayer*, 195–6.
19. Matthew 26:38.
20. Matthew 26:40.
21. John 10:30.
22. Matthew 8:4, Mark 8:26
23. Henri Nouwen, *The Inner Voice of Love* (New York: Image Books, Doubleday, 1998), 4.
24. Willard, *Spirit of the Disciplines*, 188.
25. Cecil Calvin Richardson, "The Navajo Way," *Arizona Highways*, April 1995, Vol. 71, No. 4, p. 4.
26. Foster, *Celebration of Discipline*, 145–6.

CHAPTER 11: THE DELIGHT OF HEAVEN

1. Revelation 19:9, 10; Revelation 22:8,9.
2. Sayers, *Creed or Chaos?* 29.
3. Psalm 99:5.
4. Matthew 4:10; John 4:23–24; Romans 12:1,2; Acts: 18:13; Acts:24:14; Philippians 3:3; Revelation 4:10; Revelation 22:9.
5. Peterson, *Living the Message*, 74.
6. John 1:3.
7. Acts 17:28.
8. MacDonald, *Discovering the Character of God*, 78.
9. Psalm 68:4.
10. Psalm 64:4.
11. Psalm 66:5.
12. Psalm 63:2, Psalm 65:5.
13. Romans 12:1.
14. Willard, *Spirit of the Disciplines*, 177.

15. Hebrews 12:2.
16. Psalm 84:3.
17. 2 Corinthians 6:10.
18. 1 Peter 1:6.
19. 1 Peter 1:12.
20. Oswald Chambers, *Still Higher for His Highest* (Grand Rapids: Zondervan Publishing House, 1970), 199.
21. Piper, *Godward Life*, 21.
22. Sayers, *Creed or Chaos?* 9.
23. Ibid., 10.
24. Psalm 5:11 [italics mine].
25. Psalm 68:3.
26. Nehemiah 8:10.
27. Nehemiah 8:12.
28. MacDonald, *Discovering the Character of God*, 98.
29. Proverbs 31:25.
30. Hebrews 1:9.
31. Isaiah 61:1–3.
32. Piper, *Future Grace*, 105.
33. Psalm 100:5.
34. MacDonald, *Discovering the Character of God*, 188.

CHAPTER 12: LIVING IN THE REALITY OF THE INVISIBLE

1. Hebrews 11:1.
2. 2 Corinthians 4:18.
3. Johnston, *The Cloud of Unknowing*, 56.
4. Philippians 2:13.
5. John of the Cross, *You Set My Spirit Free* (Minneapolis: Bethany House Publishers, 1994), 27.
6. Bielecki, *Teresa of Avila*, 24.
7. MacDonald, *Knowing the Heart of God*, 43.
8. Nouwen, *Inner Voice of Love*, 38.

9. Grace Jantzen, *Julian of Norwich* (New York: Paulist Press, 1987), 205.

10. DiGangi, *Golden Treasury of Puritan Devotion*, 16.

11. Manning, *Abba's Child*, 53–4.

12. Jantzen, *Julian of Norwich*, 212.

13. Yushi Nomura, *Desert Wisdom* (Maryknoll, New York: Orbis Books, 1982), 17.

14. Guyon, Madame, *Final Steps in Christian Maturity* (Sargent, Georgia: The SeedSowers, 6.

15. Romans 8:39.

16. Jantzen, *Julian of Norwich*, 214.

17. Nouwen, *Inner Voice of Love*, 102.

18. Isaiah 62:5; Matthew 25:1–13.

19. 1 John 3:1.

20. Bielecki, *Teresa of Avila*, 20.

21. MacDonald, *Discovering the Character of God*, 76.

22. John 3:35 MSG.

23. MacDonald, *Discovering the Character of God*, 212.

24. Bielecki, *Teresa of Avila*, 26.

25. Philippians 2:12.

26. Arnold, *Discipleship: Living for Christ in the Daily Grind*, 101.

27. John of the Cross, *You Set My Spirit Free*, 26.

28. Philippians 4:19.

29. Bielecki, *Teresa of Avila*, 104–5.

30. Colossians 2:2–3.

Also available from Warner Books

MENDING YOUR HEART IN A BROKEN WORLD
Finding Comfort in the Scriptures
by Patsy Clairmont

No one lifts our spirits better than bestselling author and inspirational speaker Patsy Clairmont, and no one can better help us find the spiritual glue to fix a "broken heart." In this honest, funny, and endearing book, Patsy helps us face our fears by revealing her own: the depression and anxieties that once kept her a virtual prisoner in her own home. She shows us the road to recovery with warm words that light up the darkness with the power of faith—and her down-to-earth wisdom and guidance become the best "heart menders" of all.

"Delightful . . . her exuberant spirit shines on every hope-filled page!"
—LIZ CURTIS HIGGS, BESTSELLING AUTHOR OF *BAD GIRLS OF THE BIBLE*

SISTER WIT
Devotions for Women
by Jacqueline Jakes

A leading African-American columnist who has survived a brain tumor, Jacqueline Jakes knows all too well how God gives us challenges—large and small—every day. Now she offers more than one hundred devotions to help other women handle life's difficulties, from the landmark events to the daily annoyances that test our faith. Addressing the particular needs of women and filled with uplifting quotations and anecdotes, *Sister Wit* shows us how to overcome past hurts, deal with conflicting emotions, and open our eyes to new perspectives.

"My prayer is that you will find something here to warm your heart, feed your spirit, and nourish your soul. Drink, my sisters."
—JACQUELINE JAKES, FROM THE INTRODUCTION

More . . .

A TREASURY OF MIRACLES FOR WOMEN
True Stories of God's Presence Today
by Karen Kingsbury

Created especially for women, here is a heartwarming collection of true stories about wondrous events in the lives of ordinary mothers, daughters, sisters, wives, and friends. Inspirational author Karen Kingsbury has gathered together more than a dozen tales about women of all ages whose lives have been touched by the miraculous. With each of the stories in this poignant and uplifting volume, Kingsbury reminds us that with faith, hope is never lost . . . and with love, anything is possible.

"If you have a friend who needs a ray of encouragement, take her a cup of tea and [this book]. It is indeed a treasure chest full of true stories that proves God still answers prayers today."

—PATRICIA HICKMAN, AUTHOR OF *SANDPEBBLES*